The Anatomy
of a Church

The Anatomy
of a Church

by
John MacArthur, Jr.

WORD OF GRACE COMMUNICATIONS
P.O. Box 4000
Panorama City, CA 91412

Library of Congress Cataloging in Publication Data

MacArthur, John F.
  The antatomy of a church.

  (John MacArthur's Bible studies)
  Includes index.
    1. Church—Biblical teaching.   2. Bible.   N.T.—
Criticism, interpretation, etc.   I. Title.   II. Series:
MacArthur, John F.   Bible studies.
BS2545.C5M3   1986   262   86-17997
ISBN   0-8024-5132-2   (pbk.)

2 3 4 5 6 7 Printing/EP/Year 91 90 89 88 87

Contents

These Bible studies are taken from messages delivered by Pastor-Teacher John MacArthur, Jr., at Grace Community Church in Panorama City, California. These messages have been combined into a 8-tape album entitled *The Anatomy of a Church*. You may purchase this series either in an attractive vinyl cassette album or as individual cassettes. To purchase these tapes, request the album *The Anatomy of a Church* or ask for the tapes by their individual GC numbers. Please consult the current price list; then, send your order, making your check payable to:

WORD OF GRACE COMMUNICATIONS
P.O. Box 4000
Panorama City, CA 91412

Or call the following toll-free number:
1-800-55-GRACE

1
The Anatomy of a Church—
Part 1
(The Skeleton)

Outline

Introduction
A. The Analysis
    1. The growth
    2. The goal
    3. The generations
B. The Anxiety
    1. About callousness
       a) Commitment to God
       b) Conversation about God
       c) Consideration of God
    2. About criticism
    3. About complacency
    4. About commitment

Lesson
I. The Skeleton
A. A High View of God
    1. The priority
    2. The problem
       a) Specified
       b) Solved
B. The Absolute Authority of Scripture
    1. Undermining God's Word
    2. Upholding God's Word
C. Sound Doctrine
    1. Explained
    2. Exemplified
D. Personal Holiness
    1. A concern expressed
    2. A commitment exhorted

Introduction

When I go on a trip to preach in other places, I use my time to talk with people, pray to the Lord, and read books. I also find that during a trip I am able to put aside the pressures of my regular ministry and think clearly. At times like that, the Lord impresses upon my heart certain things that are important for me to understand and to share with the people I minister to. During a recent trip, the Lord placed on me a concern for Grace Church. That church is the heart and soul of my life. Although I've been there since 1969, I still feel like the ministry there has just begun. I believe there is an exciting future before the church, a future filled with joy, anticipation, and potential. But I also believe that we are faced with a crisis. How we handle that crisis will determine the kind of future we will have.

During a recent vacation, I was playing golf with another pastor. He desired to build up his church and asked me some questions about that. He asked, "Is it difficult for you to pastor a church as large and active as yours? Now that your church is established, are you able to rest?" I told him, "Being a part of building a church is easy. It's like sitting in a sailboat while someone else blows it along." Let me explain.

A. The Analysis

   1. The growth

      I can honestly say that when Grace Church was experiencing remarkable growth, many wonderful things happened. That was an exciting, euphoric time for the church. I like to call that time the years of discovery. When I came to Grace Church, I didn't know much. Every week, I'd study and prepare my sermons, and on Sundays the congregation would learn together with me. I'd share what the Bible said, and people would say, "Wow! So that's what the Bible is saying!" We were taking big steps in terms of our spiritual growth and understanding, and the Lord added many people to the church. There was enthusiasm and energy everywhere. Even though we are doing many things now that we didn't do in those years, everything seemed just marvelous.

2. The goal

   When I first arrived at the church, my goal was to keep the people already there from leaving. I thought that if I could accomplish that, then that would be a moral victory! I never envisioned that the church would grow to the size it is now. That's why I say that the verse that I have come to appreciate the most in the years of my ministry is Ephesians 3:20: "Now unto Him who is able to do exceedingly abundantly above all that we ask or think." I have seen God do much more than I could ever imagine.

3. The generations

   During Grace Church's early years, everybody was excited and very sacrificial. An individual on the church staff recently told me, "The history of a church and its people seem to always follow an interesting pattern. The first generation fights to discover and establish the truth." Grace Church went through that; the early years were a time of discovering and establishing the truth. He continued, "The second generation fights to maintain the truth and proclaim it." We have seen that at Grace Church. The things we have learned, we have put in books and on tapes. We have trained men to become pastors, go out, and begin teaching other people. We have shared what we know with other pastors. We want to maintain and proclaim the truth. Then the staff person said, "But the third generation couldn't care less about all that." Why? Since they weren't a part of the fight the first two generations faced, they don't have anything at stake. They tend to take for granted the things that have already been established.

B. The Anxiety

1. About callousness

   That really scares me. I told my golfing companion that the toughest thing to deal with in the ministry is indifference. It's heartbreaking to know that there is a tendency for those who weren't a part of the building of the church to take everything for granted. Because they weren't a part of the battle, they neither paid the price nor enjoyed the sweet taste of victory. They don't know what the battle was like. The thing I fear is that those who weren't a part of the process of fighting, discovering, and establishing the truth will not be able to appreciate what God has done.

In Deuteronomy 6, we read that God knew the Israelites might eventually forget all that He had done for them. First, they were reminded of the need for commitment.

a) Commitment to God

God, in His wonderful grace, chose Israel to be His people. In His mercy, He brought them out of bondage in Egypt and put them in the Promised Land. He literally inundated them with divine grace and blessing. In Deuteronomy 6:3-5, He tells them, "Hear therefore, O Israel, and observe to do it, that it may be well with thee, and that ye may increase mightily, as the Lord God of thy fathers hath promised thee, in the land that floweth with milk and honey. Hear, O Israel: The Lord our God is one Lord: And thou shalt love the Lord thy God with all thine heart, and with all thy soul, and with all thy might." In other words, God was saying, "Israel, if you are going to hold true to the faith, you must love Me with all your heart, soul, and might."

You are to love God in the same way. You are to love Him more than you love your car, house, job, money, wardrobe, or anything else. I once read a convicting book by twelfth-century French churchman Bernard of Clairvaux, entitled *On the Love of God*. He said, "I have three great desires in my soul: to remember God, to contemplate God, and to love God." How many of us are like that? If we were asked to list the three great desires of our souls, I wonder if those are what they would be.

So God told Israel, "I put you in a land with milk and honey. I put you in the best place of blessing. You are going to need within you a commitment to love Me." God told them they would have to show their love for Him outwardly, too, by their conversation.

b) Conversation about God

God says in Deuteronomy 6:6-7, "And these words, which I command thee this day, shall be in thine heart; and thou shalt teach them diligently unto thy children, and shalt talk of them when thou sittest in thine house, and when thou walkest by the way, and when thou liest down, and when thou risest up."

4

What are your conversations like? Do you talk about God, Christ, the Holy Spirit, the Bible, or virtue? Do you talk about things that are good, honest, pure, and lovely? Have you ever gone on a trip with somebody for a weekend and *not* talked about God, spiritual things, or what you are accountable for? If we want to keep God's blessings, we must love God with all of our hearts and talk about Him. I believe one reason God has allowed Christian radio and tape ministries to develop is to help offset the onslaught of godlessness that comes through radio and television. Formerly society wasn't bombarded with all that garbage. People used to talk to each other in their homes. Now they have the whole world continuously talking to them about godless things. That makes it difficult for a Christian to make it from Sunday to Sunday without falling away from his commitment to God. To offset the godless things we hear and see today, we are to cultivate pure minds and talk about God.

c) Consideration of God

In Deuteronomy 6:8-9, God tells the Israelites to use symbols to remind them of Him and His commandments: "And thou shalt bind them for a sign upon thine hand, and they shall be as frontlets between thine eyes. And thou shalt write them upon the posts of thy house, and on thy gates." I believe that we should have things in our homes and offices that will make us remember what we should be thinking about. We need reminders about us to help us remember our life commitment. We should love God, talk about Him, and be reminded of Him and His commands by certain symbols around us.

You ask, "Why did God say all of that?" Deuteronomy 6:10-12 explains why: "And it shall be, when the Lord thy God shall have brought thee into the land which he swore unto thy fathers, to Abraham, to Isaac, and to Jacob, to give thee great and goodly cities, which thou buildedst not, and houses full of all good things, which thou filledst not, and wells digged, which thou diggedst not, vineyards and olive trees, which thou plantedst not, when thou shalt have eaten and be full; then beware lest thou forget the Lord."

5

I fear that some of the people who were a part of the building process at Grace Church will forget the way they saw God's work being done. Also there are many new people coming to church who don't understand the sacrifice of time, talent, effort, and money that people made while the church was growing. At that time a young couple forfeited their honeymoon because they wanted to give sacrificially. That is one of many illustrations of sacrifice I could give. People who haven't been a part of the struggle involved in church growth take for granted what has already been established. They become picky about little things that go wrong. The book *When I Relax I Feel Guilty* says they are the ones who are rearranging the chairs on the desk of the *Titanic* while it is sinking (Tim Hansel [Elgin, Ill.: David C. Cook, 1979], p. 38). Some people spend much of their time focusing on trivial things when they should be more concerned about God's kingdom.

2. About criticism

The child of apathy is criticism. It is easy for a person to come to the point where he takes everything for granted and begins to criticize any imperfections he finds. Author Thomas Hardy said he had a friend who could go into any beautiful meadow and immediately find a manure pile. A person shouldn't have that kind of perspective.

3. About complacency

God has given Grace Church many wonderful people, and we thank Him for that. But I know there are also people who come to church only when it's convenient. For them, going to church is low on the priority list. If they can't afford to go anywhere for a weekend, they come to church. They don't see any need for commitment. Soren Kierkegaard said people think that the preacher is an actor and they are to come and be his critics when in reality they're the actors and he's the prompter offstage reminding them of their lost lines (*Parables of Kierkegaard*, Thomas C. Oden, ed. [N.J.: Princeton U., 1978], pp. 89-90).

It is easy for people to reach the point where they expect things to be done for them. Even Christians have that attitude. They show up for church only if they think they will get something out of it. They don't understand the loyalty of supporting a pastor while he is speaking.

I said to my golfing friend, "Building a church is easy. The hard work begins after the church has grown. It's hard to prevent people from becoming complacent and taking everything for granted." The teaching and the music we have is great, and there are people who work hard to take care of our children during the worship service. It's easy for us to take them for granted.

4. About commitment

Many people don't even pray as they should. Do you pray for your pastor? I am very grateful for the friends I have who pray regularly for me. I know that when I preach, some of you are grading me on a scale of one to ten. If you think the sermon was good, then that might be enough to make you come back for another good sermon. But do you pray for me? Do you pray for those who lead and serve you? Some are quick to criticize but not so quick to pray. Do those of you in a leadership position in your church pray for the people you lead? Or do you think that everything is going along well enough and you don't need God anymore?

Some people don't understand the warfare involved in building up a church. They just see all the good things that result from tears and toil and take them for granted. Some people don't understand that the leaders of a church have to hold up each other because the battle against indifference becomes so difficult. They need you to be a part of what's going on. They need you to be totally committed and prayerful. They need you to use your gifts and serve the church.

A Victim of Apathy

I received a letter from a young pastor that I would like to share with you. My greatest joy in the ministry is to see young men go into the ministry. This letter is from a young man who is thinking about leaving the ministry, and it broke my heart. This is what he wrote:

> This letter comes to your attention for several reasons, and although we have not met personally, I have read some of your books and heard you on the radio several times. Let me explain to you something I'm concerned about that I have not been able to correct.

It is causing me to consider leaving the ministry. Perhaps the Lord will use your insights to give me some light.

I firmly believe that the leaders of a church should be the very best, not only in their personal spiritual lives but also in being examples for the people they lead. I am not saying that a leader has to be perfect or superhuman, but he should have a living, growing personal relationship with our Lord. I firmly believe that if the leaders of a church don't present a life-style of commitment and dedication to their Lord and church, then their followers won't either.

The problem, pastor MacArthur, is that two-thirds of our elected officers attend only one service a week. I'm not saying they all have to be present every time the doors are open, but I do believe that, excepting unforeseen situations, illnesses, and vacations, the leadership of a church should make a double effort to be present at the services, if for no other reason than for the encouragement of the saints and the pastor. I find it extremely difficult to believe that proper leadership can be provided when the leaders do not spend enough time with their people to find out what their hurts and fears are. At our board meetings, I find that by far the majority of the time is spent on items that have no direct relationship to the needs and hurts of people. I believe that because of that, our church has come to a stalemate, which is equal to going backwards instead of moving ahead. I have brought those things to the attention of our board on several occasions (even some of the people on our board are not faithful in their attendance), with absolutely no results.

I am not talking about men and women who simply are not able to make it to church, but people who just will not come. Some of the leaders say they are too busy, are too tired at the end of the day, or don't even offer an excuse. But those leaders are not afraid to remind me that they are the power of the church. That happens often. I have come to the place where if this continues on into next year, I am ready to resign the pastorate. How is it possible for a pastor to direct his flock, establish the needed programs, and develop spiritual leadership if he can't get other leaders to back him? I'm open to your advice. I believe our church has great possibilities. But as long as we are luke-warm, the Lord will not bless us or use us.

That letter could have been written by thousands of pastors, because it is common for people to take for granted the good things God has given them. I don't want that to happen at Grace Church. I don't want people to forget the Lord. I want them to continue to fear His name.

Look with me at 2 Peter 1:12. Writing to his congregation, Peter said, "Wherefore, I will not be negligent to put you always in remembrance of these things, though ye know them, and are established in the present truth." Peter had a high calling from God, and he didn't want to be irresponsible. He didn't want to be negligent concerning those he was called to teach, so he continually reminded the people of the things they had already learned. He was saying, "I know that you already know these things, but you need to be reminded of them." Continuing in verse 13, he says, "Yea, I think it fitting, as long as I am in this tabernacle, to stir you up by putting you in remembrance, knowing that shortly I must put off this my tabernacle. . . . I will endeavor that ye may be able, after my decease, to have these things always in remembrance" (vv. 13-15). There is a certain virtue in repeating basic facts that shouldn't be forgotten. That is what I'd like to do now as I share with you what is on my heart.

Many pastors come to Grace Church to find out why it grows and what we are doing. They usually come to find out how things are done. They desire to know what God is doing, and some of them think they can pick up methods, tools, programs, and ideas and apply them to their own churches. However, that is like coming to pick up a body and going back home with just the skin. They are looking for the flesh of our ministries, not the internal aspects beneath them. Below the surface is a foundation that people don't know about. We try to tell pastors that. They may see a ministry functioning, but it is what is behind the scenes that needs to be understood.

For our study, I am going to use the analogy of a body the apostle Paul uses in 1 Corinthians 12:12-31, and entitle this series "The Anatomy of a Church." A body has four main features: skeleton, internal systems, muscles, and flesh. A church needs to have a framework (a skeleton), internal systems (certain attitudes), muscles (different functions), and flesh (the form of the programs). The form cannot be reproduced without the other features of the body. Borrowing then from Paul's familiar metaphor, I want to talk first about the skeleton.

Lesson

I. THE SKELETON

In order for the body to function, it has to have structure. The skeleton is what gives a body structure. I believe there are certain skeletal truths that a church must be committed to. They are unalterable; they cannot be compromised in any way. When I say that a church has to be committed to those things, I am talking about you and me. You and I are the church. The first nonnegotiable requirement of a church is that it have:

A. A High View of God

It is absolutely essential that a church perceive itself as an institution for the glory of God. I believe that the church in America has descended from that and become a church that focuses on men. The church thinks its goal is to help people feel better about themselves: It plays psychological games with people and gives them placebos. But placebos aren't the answer.

1. The priority

The church has been reduced from an organism that emphasizes knowing and glorifying God to an organization that tries to help people feel better about themselves. But if you know and glorify God, then you *will* feel better about yourself. If you know God, the needs in your life are met. "The fear of the Lord is the beginning of wisdom" (Prov. 9:10). When you have a right relationship with God, everything else will fall into its proper place. I am not saying that we are to ignore people's needs. We are to be concerned about people as God is. But a balance must be found, and that begins with a high view of God.

Sometimes I wish God would strike people dead during the offering. I don't wish that too strongly, but I wish something dramatic would happen to show people that they must take God seriously. When a person dies, we have a tendency to say, "How could God let that happen?" We have no right to ask that. We should ask, "What are we doing alive?" The Lord, being holy, could have destroyed man when he first fell into sin. Just because God is gracious toward us is no excuse for us to be indifferent. God must be taken seriously.

2. The problem

    a) Specified

    I feel righteous indignation toward preachers and others who take God off His throne and turn Him into a servant who has to do all the things they demand of Him. People are irreverent today; they do not know how to worship God. Some think that worship means to induce a warm feeling. They know little about God. There are too many Marthas and not enough Marys (Luke 10:38-42). We are so busy serving that we don't take time to bow down and wash Jesus' feet. We don't tremble at God's Word. We don't allow ourselves to be confronted by God's holiness and our sinfulness so that we can be usable to Him for His glory. We want to feel good about ourselves. We want to have our needs met and problems solved, and we allow the church to be replaced by religious psychology.

You could take most of the books that are being written today, throw them into the sea, and not lose anything. Many are just placebos that superficially attack problems that people can't solve. During the eras when the church was holy, Christians had very few books to read, but the books they did have told them how to have a relationship with God. Most books today don't do that. A survey taken at a recent Moody Bible Institute pastor's conference revealed that most pastors need help in dealing with families. I was amazed. I said, "You mean to tell me that even with all the books available about helping families, that's still a problem area?" The answer isn't to write more materials about the family; the problem is that people aren't taking God seriously and walking according to His laws. It's so important to have a high view of God.

b) Solved

James 4:8 says, "Draw near to God, and he will draw near to you." Would you like to live your life with God near you? If you draw close to God, He will come close to you. But you say, "When I get near God, it is easy to become nervous." That's why James 4:8 also says, "Cleanse your hands, ye sinners." The closer you get to God, the more you see your sin. Consequently, you will humble yourself and mourn over it. James 4:10 says that when you have humbled yourself before the Lord, "he shall lift you up."

We must take God seriously and exalt Him; we don't want to have a man-centered church. We are to reach out to everyone in the love of Christ, but God is to be the focus of our worship and our life. Therefore, we shouldn't look at the Bible as a book full of formulas for solving problems; it is a book that reveals God.

The second nonnegotiable truth is that a church must believe in:

B. The Absolute Authority of Scripture

1. Undermining God's Word

The Bible is constantly being attacked. A seminary professor recently wrote a book that says it is all right for two men to have a homosexual relationship. If a person wants to advocate that view, all he has to do is disregard the Bible. It is inconsistent for a seminary professor to deny the Bible when he is training men to minister the Word of God. But that is happening today. The Bible is being attacked head on.

People attack the Bible when they add visions and revelations to it. Some say that Jesus told them this and that God told them that. In the meantime, they are subtly undermining the Bible because they no longer see it as the single authority. One man said that Jesus comes into his bathroom and puts His arm around him while he is shaving. I thought, *Do you keep on shaving? If you can keep on shaving, then it isn't Jesus!* It is an awesome thing to confront an infinitely holy God. Getting such special messages from God is silliness. God's Word must be held up as the absolute authority.

The Bible is always attacked. The worst attack of all is by people who say they believe the Bible, yet don't know what it teaches. That is the subtlest kind of attack. There are people across America who say, "I believe the Bible from cover to cover," but they don't know one paragraph of it. The believe what they don't know.

2. Upholding God's Word

Jesus said, "Man shall not live by bread alone, but by every word that proceedeth out of the mouth of God" (Matt. 4:4). If we are fed by every word that comes out of the mouth of God, then we ought to study every word. Today, many things are preached except the Word of God. We must teach the Bible—every word of it. That is important, and it doesn't matter if you don't have an appetite for it.

You say, "I don't need another sermon; I'd rather be fellowshiping." I hope you enjoy your fellowship, but I'm going to keep on feeding you the Word of God, because that's what makes you grow. Fellowship is important, but it does not replace the Word of God. In fact, I find that the sweetest, purest, and most rewarding fellowship is always with the Scripture. That's where my heart is. I hope that's where your heart is, too. You say, "We already know much of what the Bible says. We have been taught for a long time." But to say something like that is the height of pride. The discovery process never stops—I'm always learning new things from the Bible. The greatest joy of my preaching ministry is to study the Bible and discover things I never saw before. Every week of my life I learn something new from the Word that I never fully understood before. That's an adventure that no one should miss.

A pastor once told me, "I pastor a church for only two years, and then I leave." I said, "Have you been doing that for a long time?" He said, "Yes. I spent two years here, two years there, and two years in another place." I said, "Why?" He said, "I have fifty-two sermons. I preach each one twice, and then I leave." I said, "Why don't you teach the whole counsel of God?" He said, "I don't teach all of it; I just teach the parts that I think are important." But every word that proceeds out of the mouth of God is important.

The third thing that a church must have as a part of its skeleton is:

C. Sound Doctrine

1. Explained

If you have a high view of God and are committed to Him, then you must go along with what His Word teaches. The teachings of God's Word make up sound doctrine. Many Christians today are vague about doctrine. There are many of what I call "sermonettes for Christianettes"—little sermons that are nice and interesting. Sometimes they make you feel warm, fuzzy, sad, or excited. But seldom do we hear doctrine taught or discussed. Very few explain the truths about God, life, death, heaven, hell, man, sin, Christ, angels, the Holy Spirit, the position of the believer, the flesh, or the world. We need truths that we can hold onto. That's why it's so important to understand the principles of the Bible. You read a text, find out what it says and means, draw out a divine truth, and establish that truth in the minds of others by repeating it. That's what I do when I preach. I go through a Bible passage, pull out a divine truth, teach about it using other passages, and explain that truth several different ways until it's established in the hearers' minds.

I picked up that style of preaching when I graduated from high school. My father gave me a Bible and wrote a note in it encouraging me to read 1 and 2 Timothy. I did that, and Paul's message to Timothy kept running through my mind: "If thou put the brethren in remembrance of these things, thou shalt be a good minister of Jesus Christ, nourished up in the words of faith and of good doctrine, unto which thou hast attained" (1 Tim. 4:6; cf. 1 Tim. 1:3, 10; 4:13, 16).

2. Exemplified

Earlier in my ministry at Grace Church, I taught from the book of Ephesians, explaining a believer's position in Christ. That study was foundational to the church. Recently I visited with my high school football coach, whom I hadn't seen for a long time. He is a Christian and also teaches the Word of God—he's a wonderful man. We were reminiscing about some of the silly things that happened when I played football in high school. Then he said to me, "John, you have made concrete for me the position of the believer in Christ. I have listened to your tapes on Ephesians chapter one many times and taught from that passage repeatedly over the years to young people. Understanding the doctrine of the believer's position in Jesus Christ has given me a foundation for my entire life."

I didn't give my coach that foundation; the book of Ephesians and the Holy Spirit did. My point is that people need solid doctrine on which to build their lives. I believe we must make principles from the divine truths of the Word of God and teach them, for they are foundational to the Christian life. For example, if you want to learn about angels or demons, then find out what the Bible teaches about them. Learning the solid content of the Bible is important.

The fourth nonnegotiable thing that the people of a church should have is:

D. Personal Holiness

1. A concern expressed

We are all victimized by an absolutely unholy society. I cringe when I think of the philosophical and immoral filth that our society creates. Peoples' minds are corrupted

14

and drawn away from God as a result. That filth is like the drippings of a broken sewer. In fact, the sewer isn't just broken; it's completely shattered and letting loose a flood. For example, I have a problem with contemporary music not only because I don't like the style of it but because the sexual innuendos of the words are so vile. I try to explain that to young people and many say, "You don't understand; you're old. What do you know? The words are all right; I take them the way I want."

We have to draw lines when it comes to personal holiness and be careful what we expose ourselves and our children to. It is impossible to watch some of the films in theaters and to read trash without paying a price. I stay away from most movies so that I don't have to be exposed to such worldliness. Christians are called to live a pure life, and we can't compromise that. We should enforce a standard of purity among ourselves.

2. A commitment exhorted

    Second Corinthians 7:1 says, "Having, therefore, these promises, dearly beloved, let us cleanse ourselves from all filthiness of the flesh and spirit, perfecting holiness in the fear of God." A church should enforce that standard (see Matt. 18:15-17). That's why we implement church discipline at Grace Church. If somebody sins, we confront him.

    Many Christians aren't as concerned about their personal holiness as they should be. A person's prayer life is one of the things that cultivates holiness. What is your prayer life like? What about your study of the Word of God? Do you fast? How often do you meditate on the Word of God, if at all? You say, "I'm an elder," or, "I'm a deacon, and I teach a Bible study." I'm not talking about that; I'm asking, "How often do you meditate for a prolonged period of time, drawing nigh unto God in a prayer that extends beyond the moment? Where are you in terms of holiness and real communion with the living God?" Church leaders aren't the only people that should live holy lives. I should live a holy life, the leaders of a church should live holy lives, and you should live a holy life. We can't live half-committed Christian lives and expect God's work to be done.

The last thing I want to mention that belongs in the skeletal structure of a church is:

15

E. Spiritual Authority

1. The office of spiritual leaders explained

A church must understand that Christ is the head of the church (Eph. 1:22; 4:15) and that He mediates His rule in the church through godly elders (1 Thess. 5:12-13; Heb. 13:7, 17). The Bible teaches that; I didn't invent it. The Bible says that elders have the rule over the congregation in the Lord. They have authority.

That authority can be abused. There are men who wield it as if it were given to them. But they are not the actual authorities. They are simply supposed to handle the authority of the Word of God. I don't have the authority to tell Grace Church, "Put that building over there," "I want more vacations," "Raise my salary," or, "I demand that those walls be painted green." The only authority I have is to speak and apply the Word of God. When a spiritual leader goes outside of that, then he is going beyond the bounds of his authority.

2. The obedience to spiritual leaders expected

If you were to do something wrong and continue doing it, that would be disastrous. It is important to confess a wrongdoing. The role of a spiritual leader is to help people get back on the right track and move on for the glory of the Lord. First Thessalonians 5 says to "know them who labor among you, and are over you in the Lord, and admonish you, and to esteem them very highly in love for their work's sake" (vv. 12-13). Hebrews 13:7, 17 says to submit to those over you in the Lord, for they watch your souls. Follow their example.

3. The operation of spiritual leaders exemplified

We have many leaders at Grace Church; I'm just one of them. You say, "Why is it that you are the one who always preaches?" That's just the way the gifts work out. Jesus had twelve apostles. Every time there is a list of them, Peter's name is first (Matt. 10:2-4; Mark 3:16-19; Luke 6:14-16; Acts 1:13). He was always the spokesman. That doesn't mean he was better than the others. He simply had the gift of speaking, and the others were gifted in other ways.

Peter and John always traveled together. Because of that, you would think that John didn't say much. But he wrote the gospel of John, 1, 2, and 3 John, and Revelation.

16

There is no doubt that with the intimate friendship he had with Christ, he could have shared more great things. But every time he was with Peter in the first twelve chapters of Acts, he was silent. Why? Because Peter had the gift of speaking. Barnabas was a great teacher, one of the leading ones in the early church. But when Barnabas and Paul traveled together, even unbelievers professed that Paul was the chief speaker.

So there are variations in the giftedness of spiritual leaders. But in totality, there is still an equality of spritiual authority given to those that the Bible calls elders, or overseers.

Let's sum up what we've learned. If the church is going to be the Body of Christ, it has to have the right framework. It has to have a high view of God. The pursuit of a church should be to know God. In seeking to know God, the authority of the Scripture must be recognized, for it is through the Bible that we can know God. A church should have a high view of Scripture and a commitment to teaching sound doctrine. The people of a church should also seek personal holiness and submit their souls to the care of those the Lord has placed over them as spiritual authorities.

Focusing on the Facts

1. Describe the characteristics of each of the three generations of a church (see p. 3).
2. Why is it easy for the third generation of people at a church to be apathetic (see p. 3)?
3. What was God telling Israel in Deuteronomy 6:3-5? How does that apply to us (see p. 4)?
4. According to Deuteronomy 6:6-7, where were the Israelites to keep God's words? To whom were they to teach God's Word? How often were they to converse about God (see p. 4)?
5. Why may have God allowed Christian radio and tape ministries to develop (see p. 5)?
6. What was God's command to the Israelites in Deuteronomy 6:8-9? How can we apply that today (see p. 5)?
7. According to Deuteronomy 6:10-12, why did God command the Israelites all that He did in Deuteronomy 6:3-9 (see p. 5)?
8. Kierkegaard said, "Some people think that the preacher is an actor and they are to come and be his critics." What, in reality, is the situation (see p. 6)?
9. Some people are quick to _____ and not so quick to _____ (see p. 7).
10. What was Peter's message in 2 Peter 1:12? Explain it (see p. 9).

11. What are the four main features of a body? Relate those features to the church (see p. 9).
12. What are the five nonnegotiable necessities of a church's structure (see pp. 10-16)?
13. The church must perceive itself as _____. In general, what have churches in America descended to (see p. 10)?
14. What happens when a person makes a priority of glorifying God and having a right relationship with Him (see p. 10)?
15. Explain the specific problem that many churches and Christians have today. Why is that occurring (see pp. 10-11)?
16. According to James 4:10, what does God do to people who in humility cleanse themselves of sin (see p. 11)?
17. In what ways is the Bible being attacked today (see p. 12)?
18. What does Matthew 4:4 say about God's Word? What place does fellowship have in relation to the study of the Word of God (see pp. 12-13)?
19. What is sound doctrine (see p. 13)?
20. Why do Christians need to be taught sound doctrine (see p. 14)?
21. How are people's minds affected by the philosophical and immoral filth that our society creates? How must Christians respond to that kind of influence (see pp. 14-15)?
22. Describe the standard that a Christian should have (2 Cor. 7:1). What is one of the things that cultivate personal holiness (see p. 15)?
23. Who is the head of the church? Through whom does the head of the church mediate rule over the church? Support your answers with Scripture (see p. 16).
24. Are spiritual leaders the actual authorities of a church? Explain. What does a spiritual leader have the authority to do (see p. 16)?
25. What is one role of a spiritual leader? What commands are given to us in 1 Thessalonians 5:12-13 and Hebrews 13:7, 17 in regard to spiritual leaders (see p. 16)?
26. Despite the variations in the giftedness of spiritual leaders, what is true about their authority (see p. 17)?

Pondering the Principles

1. Read about the different generations of a church on page 3. Which generation is your church in right now? If your church is working now to discover and establish the truth, are you helping it along with that? What is your attitude toward learning the truths of the Bible and making them foundational to your church and personal life? If your church is fighting to maintain and proclaim the truth, are you actively helping the church with

those goals? Does your life display a continual obedience to God's Word? Are you involved in teaching or communicating the gospel with others? If you go to a church that is well established and has excellent programs, are you actively involved in those programs? Do you take time to pray for those who work hard behind the scenes? How much commitment do you have to your church? Take time now to evaluate where your church is in terms of its growth. What can you do to help it be all that it should be?

2. Bernard of Clairvaux said, "I have three great desires in my soul: to remember God, to contemplate God, and to love God." Can you honestly say that you have those same desires? Do you show your love for God? How? Ask God to help you focus on Him in the way that you should.

3. There are five foundational things that a church must be committed to: a high view of God, a belief in the absolute authority of Scripture, a commitment to teaching sound doctrine, the personal holiness of its people, and the establishment of spiritual leaders. Of the five items listed above, take one item at a time and explain what problems could arise if that item was missing in a church. Are there any of those problems in your church? Determine what you can do to help.

2
The Anatomy of a Church—
Part 2
(The Internal Systems—Part A)

Outline

Introduction

Review
1. The Skeleton

Lesson
II. The Internal Systems
  A. Obedience
    1. The requirement to be obedient
    2. The refusal to be obedient
      a) Without an understanding of God's Word
      b) With an understanding of God's Word
    3. The references on being obedient
    4. The result of being obedient
    5. The resignation from being obedient
  B. Humility
    1. The pursuit of humility
    2. The position of humility
    3. The priority of humility
    4. The perspectives of humility
      a) A proper perspective of self
      b) A proper perspective of others
  C. Love
    1. The love of the world
    2. The love of the Word
      a) Demonstrated by the Good Samaritan
      b) Demonstrated by God's Son
  D. Unity
    1. The privation of unity
    2. The preservation of unity

a) Exemplified
b) Exhorted

Introduction

In this study on the anatomy of a church, I want to do some spiritual archaeology. I want to dig up a small part of Grace Church's foundation so that you can see the basics that Grace Church is committed to. At the same time, I am borrowing from Paul's analogy of a church as a body (1 Cor. 12:12-31). We shall look at four features of the body in this study: the skeleton, the internal systems, the muscles, and the flesh.

Review

I. THE SKELETON (see pp. 9-17)

A skeleton gives a church its framework. It helps give it support. The skeleton is what holds the body together and enables it to move.

There are five nonnegotiable, foundational principles to which a church must be committed. We must always exalt God. We should always make studying, preaching, and teaching God's Word a priority. We must be committed to learning doctrine from the Bible and communicating it accurately. With the strength we have in the Holy spirit, we are to pursue holiness. We must understand spiritual authority: those who are spiritual leaders have great responsibility, as well as those who follow.

When I preach, I frequently mention all those basic things because I want to keep reminding people of the framework that is essential in the makeup of the church. I will always go back to the basic themes of God, Scripture, doctrine, holiness, and spiritual authority. Sometimes I may seem to be repeating a past sermon, but I generally don't do that. Those things have to be repeated frequently so that when I'm gone, the people I've taught will still remember them. Peter did the same thing (2 Pet. 1:12-14). Paul said in Philippians 2:12, "Wherefore, my beloved, as ye have always obeyed, not as in my presence only but now much more in my absence, work out your own salvation with fear and trembling." I would have great satisfaction if I could someday look down from heaven and say, "The people of Grace Church are still committed to the things they were when I was there." I believe that the skeletal, nonnegotiable principles that a church should be committed to must be emphasized repeatedly by its preacher. I also believe those principles should be a part of a church's teaching ministry: If you teach a Bible study, a children's class, or disciple someone, you need to reiterate the foundational principles so that everyone in the Body of Christ will be what he should be. There must be a demonstration of commitment not only in what the people of a church say, but in the lives they live. I must live my commitment to personal holiness, doctrinal clarity, and the authority of Scripture, or my preaching would be worthless.

Lesson

II. THE INTERNAL SYSTEMS

A church must have flowing through it certain spiritual attitudes. A physical body has organs and fluids in it that keep the body alive and functioning. A skeleton gives a framework to a church but doesn't give it life. The life of a church comes from its spiritual attitudes. The goal of a pastor and other leaders of a church should be to generate proper spiritual attitudes in the people. The leaders can't just say, "You need to do this and that." They must generate the spiritual attitudes in people that will motivate them to proper behavior. A person can do something good outwardly, yet have a bad attitude. However, good outward behavior should come from good attitudes. That's why it's so important to emphasize the fruit of the Spirit (Gal. 5:22-23)—the internal attitudes.

Sometimes a young man goes into a pastorate and sees certain things missing in his church. He sees a lack of organization and becomes tempted to reorganize the church. He may say, "Let's appoint some elders and reorganize this church!" But do you know what will happen after the reorganizing is finished? He will have the same people with the same attitudes in a different structure, and the people are not going to understand the purposes of the change.

When I first came to Grace Church, I had a new idea about how to run the Sunday school. I wrote out my idea and presented it to the Education Committee. They unanimously turned it down. They said, "Who are you? We've been here longer than you." In effect, they were saying, "Prove yourself." Several years later, the Education Committee came up with the same system I had proposed. That showed me it is important to develop in people the spiritual attitudes that will bring about the right kind of responses. If the right kind of spiritual attitudes are present in a church, then the structure will take care of itself, because Spirit-controlled people are going to do Spirit-led things. They will naturally conform to the biblical pattern.

A church should work on the attitudes of its people. I'm not interested in trying to make sure the people of Grace Church behave a certain way by giving their money, coming to church Sunday mornings, Sunday evenings, and Wednesday nights; praying five hours a week; and reading the Bible every day. Those things are not to be approached on a legalistic or superficial basis. The emphasis of a ministry should be on generating proper spiritual attitudes. Sometimes that's difficult to do because some people don't want to have right attitudes, and it becomes easy to let them do "good" things with a bad attitude. But that will allow the people with bad attitudes to derive satisfaction from legalistic behavior.

Let's look at the attitudes that should be in our hearts. First of all, we should have an attitude of:

A. Obedience

    1. The requirement to be obedient

        This attitude overarches all other attitudes. An obedient person does whatever God says to do. He does not compromise. If God says something, that's it—there is nothing to argue about. It's important for us to have God's Word in our minds so that we know how to be obedient. There are several important reasons for us to live obedient lives: to glorify God, to receive blessing, to be a witness to unbelievers, and to be an example for other Christians. Being obedient also allows us to be filled with the Spirit. When we're filled with the Spirit, we're able to reach out to unbelievers and set an example for those who watch how we live.

        You say, "The fact that we should be obedient seems to be obvious." That's because you became a Christian by affirming the lordship of Jesus Christ. You said, "Jesus, You're in charge of my life now. You're Lord, and I'm Your servant." Jesus says in Luke 6:46, "And why call ye me, Lord, Lord, and do not the things which I say?" In other words, He is saying, "Don't call Me Lord, and not obey Me!" If Jesus is Lord in your life, then you should do what He asks you to do. Matthew 7:13-14 says that the path to salvation is narrow. That's because it is confined by God's will, law, and Word. We are to affirm Christ as

Lord (Rom. 10:9-10) and submit to His lordship. Doing that means living a life of obedience.

2. The refusal to be obedient

   a) Without an understanding of God's Word

   A man once sent a letter and a tape to me, sharing a matter that was on his heart. During the first ten minutes of the tape, he talked about how he listened to our radio program and appreciated the study of the Bible. Then he said he had many sins in his life that God was working on, one of which he wanted to ask me about. He said he had never had normal feelings toward women; instead, he had strong feelings toward farm animals. However, he didn't think that was a problem because he didn't feel any guilt about it. He believed that the Lord was refining him in other areas, but not in that one. A four-page letter was sent back to him explaining that his problem was a sin in the eyes of God. In fact, if he had lived in the Old Testament era, he would have been killed, for Leviticus 20:15 says, "If a man lie with a beast, he shall surely be put to death." The letter kindly expressed that God doesn't select certain sins to work on and leave others alone. Any sin is an affront to His holy name.

   Later, that man sent another tape to me. He said, "I don't think anybody understands. Christians are so tangled up in God's Word that they don't understand how God works and feels." Let me say this: How are we going to know how God feels about something if we don't read the Bible? That man didn't want to listen to what God had to say about his problem because he said he didn't feel any guilt. I wonder if he is even a Christian, because 1 John 2:5 says, "Whosoever keepeth his word, in him verily is the love of God perfected; by this know we that we are in him." If you're a Christian, then you'll keep God's commandments. A person who can have that kind of abomination in his life and say that he knows how God feels—without reading the Bible—has a problem. Sin makes a person self-justifying.

   That's an extreme illustration, but it points out the fact that God has called us to be obedient to His Word. We should know how He feels about things because He tells us in His Word. The goal of ministry should be to build an obedient people. That is what God intended to do in both the Old and New Testaments. When God speaks, we are to obey.

b) With an understanding of God's Word

It is sad that when some people are confronted with divine truth that convicts them of something in their lives that isn't right, they will continue in their pattern of disobedience. For example: Suppose you hear a sermon about forgiveness. There is somebody you know that you need to forgive, but you push that sermon out of your mind and continue to have a bitter, unforgiving spirit. That is disobedience. It is diametrically opposed to all that God wants to accomplish in your life.

3. The references on being obedient

You say, "I go to church. Isn't that enough?" First Samuel 15:22 says, "Behold, to obey is better than sacrifice." Ritual will never replace obedience. In 1 Peter 1, the apostle says that you are to "gird up the loins of your mind" (v. 13a). In other words, make sure that your priorities are right. Be "obedient children, not fashioning yourselves according to the former lusts in your ignorance" (1 Pet. 1:14). Don't live as you did before you became a Christian. You are to be an obedient child.

Jesus said, "Blessed are they that hear the word of God, and keep it" (Luke 11:28). Paul, commending some of the Roman Christians, said, "Your obedience is come abroad unto all men. I am glad" (Rom. 16:19). A pastor's heart is made happy when the obedience of his people is manifest.

4. The result of being obedient

Howard Hendricks once said something I thought was very interesting: He remarked that people who have been Christians for a long time and are over fifty years old should be the most excited, committed, purest, and servantlike people in the church. The very energy of a church ought to be from the people who are more than fifty years old. They should be the ones on the forefront in evangelism and prayer. Why? Because they've lived with God the longest. They've applied the Word to their lives for so long that they've become more obedient and

26

mature than those who have been Christians for only a few years.

I think it is wonderful that Grace Church has many young people. I like young people because they are energetic. But it's a sad thing to say that the energy of a church comes only from its young people. Often I hear young pastors say, "My church is good and is in a nice area, but it's full of old people." The old people in the church ought to be the dynamic ones.

5. The resignation from being obedient

If you're a Christian but don't apply God's Word to your life, you'll just become one of those inert older people. You'll want to retire spiritually. You'll say, "I've been going to church for many years. I don't want to get involved in evangelism; I'd rather leave that kind of thing for younger people." Look at the Old Testament leaders of Israel: Many of them were older people. The early church found its energy in the mature saints. Today, the church is deriving its energy from young people. We need the energy that young people have, but we also need the power that older believers have developed from their long, obedient lives. But because many believers don't apply what they hear as they get older, their lives don't change. They may know a lot of spiritual facts, but they have no power. I don't want that to happen in my life. I don't want to say that I ran out of energy for serving Christ by the time I was fifty years old. I think the reason many people eventually stop serving Christ is that they've heard the Bible but haven't applied it.

We must be committed to obeying God's Word. If the Spirit teaches you a truth, apply it. When you're confronted with conviction, don't say, "I wish so-and-so could have heard that sermon." Apply the sermon to yourself. When you obey Christ, you grow in spiritual maturity and become more useful to God.

The second attitude a Christian should have is:

B. Humility

1. The pursuit of humility

I've had problems with pride in the past. I'm sure that you've had problems with it, too. Humility is very elusive because when you say to yourself, "I'm humble," you're being proud.

An Uncomfortable Chair

I have always desired to help people in their understanding of humility. At Grace Church, when we built the auditorium that we now use as a gymnasium, someone ordered five big chairs with crowns at the top of their backs. Before the services started, I was supposed to sit in the chair in the middle. I tried that for a couple of weeks and didn't like it. Instead, I preferred to sit in the front row of the pew with the congregation. I didn't want people thinking I was proud of myself or better than them. Sitting in the front row of the pew gives me the same perspective as everyone else: I was in church to worship God. The only difference between my congregation and me is that God has called me to be a preacher and given me the gift of preaching. I'm not a pastor because I'm a better person than you are.

The Holy Spirit tells us through the Scripture to seek humility. We're to pursue it with the strength that God has given us.

2. The position of humility

I hope that when you became a Christian, you weren't under the illusion that God needed you. Some people say, "If the Lord could only save that person! He has such great talent and is a good leader." That's ridiculous. The Lord can save anybody He wants to save. Also, we have nothing to offer to God. We're like the man in Matthew 18:23-34 who couldn't pay his ten-thousand-talent debt. He had nothing to offer. Matthew 5:3 says, "Blessed are the poor in spirit; for theirs is the kingdom of heaven." In other words, when we came into God's kingdom, we came as destitute beggars who had nothing to offer. We were spiritually bankrupt. If we have anything now, it isn't because we earned it; God gave it to us. The only thing I have to offer back to God is what He gave me through His gift of salvation and His Spirit. I can't take any credit for what I am; I must give God the glory. I have no reason to be proud.

3. The priority of humility

The leaders of Grace Church have endeavored to withstand the preoccupation people have with self-esteem and the selfishness of our contemporary society. We point out the fact that God has called Christians to be sacrificial and humble. The Bible talks repeatedly about humility. Jesus says in effect in Matthew 16:24-25, "Let a man deny himself, take up his cross, and gain his life by following Me." He says the same thing in Matthew 10:38-39: "Deny yourself and follow Me. Pay the price of self- effacement and set yourself below others." In Philippians 2:3-4 we read, "In lowliness of mind let each esteem others better than themselves. Look not every man on his own things, but every man also on the things of others." Seek to honor other people and meet their needs. If the people of a church are fighting for positions of authority, then they are going to have the same chaos there was when all the disiciples were seeking to be the greatest (Matt. 20:20-21; Mark 9:33-35; Luke 22:24).

4. The perspectives of humility

   a) A proper perspective of self

   We should desire to be humble. That doesn't mean we are to undervalue ourselves, because in Christ we are eternally priceless. However, Christ is the One who made us priceless—we didn't do that ourselves. Humility means seeing another person as more important than yourself. We aren't to walk around saying "I'm a worm; I'm a rat; I'm a bum; I'm nothing." We're of value to God because we're redeemed and sanctified. That enables us to serve Him.

   b) A proper perspective of others

   A humble person sees others as being important. Matthew 19:19 says, "Thou shalt love thy neighbor as thyself." You are to have the same commitment to meeting your neighbor's needs as you do your own. In 1 Corinthians, Paul reprimanded the Corinthian Christians for the boastful, self-centered way that they exhibited their ecstatic experiences. They thought they were more spiritual than other Christians because of their ecstasies. God desires the people in His church to have an attitude of humility. If I have that attitude, then I'm not going to be upset if something good comes your way and not mine. You're more important than I am. To be humble means that I set aside some of my priorities to make sure your needs are met. It means that I will not do things that violate your conscience (Rom. 14:13-15). If meat or certain drinks offend you, then I won't have those things in your presence (Rom. 14:20-21), "for the kingdom of God is not food and drink, but righteousness, and peace, and joy in the Holy Spirit" (Rom. 14:17). Humility means that I'm not going to do anything that will make you stumble; I'm going to set my liberty aside. I must care for you and love you. If you drift from the flock, then I must pursue you and bring you back (Matt. 18:15-17). We're all to have the meekness and gentleness of Christ that Paul mentions in 2 Corinthians 10:1.

It has always been my desire to see the people of Grace Church be obedient to God and to have an attitude of humility rather than self-centeredness. So many problems come up when people seek their own will. Some people enjoy being told how wonderful they are; instead, they should give their lives to encourage others. The third attitude we should have is:

C. Love

1. The love of the world

Only people that are humble can show love. Now, I'm not talking about the worldly kind of love that is counterfeit and object-oriented. That's why many marriages don't last: Worldly love is only an emotion, and when the emotion is gone, the relationship is gone. The world thinks that kind of love is great because of the feelings involved. Worldly love seeks only to get and not to give.

2. The love of the Word

Biblical love is not like that. It's not an emotion. Biblical love is an act of sacrificial service. It's not an attitude; it's an action. Love always does something. The words used to describe love in 1 Corinthians 13:4-7 are all verbs. Love is an act of service on your behalf that flows out of a heart of humility. A humble person says, "I care more about you than myself," and acts out his care in love. That's why I say that only humble people can love others. Proud people can't love others because they're too busy caring for themselves. The only love they know is a physical love; they have emotional attachments to certain people. They don't care about anybody else. They enjoy being with others who are like them, and are indifferent to the needs of everybody else.

a) Demonstrated by the Good Samaritan

Biblical love meets people's needs. Jesus said in Luke 10:27, "Thou shalt love . . . thy neighbor as thy self."

Then He was asked by a lawyer, "And who is my neighbor?" (v. 29*b*). Jesus answered with the story of the Good Samaritan (Luke 10:30-37). The Samaritan was walking on a road and came upon a man who had been badly beaten. He helped him out and met his needs. Who is your neighbor? Anyone you meet who has a need. Whom are you to love? Anyone who has a need. How do you love him? Meet his need, even if you don't feel an emotional attachment or an attraction for him. Love flows from humility; the humble person considers other people more important than himself.

b) Demonstrated by God's Son

A classic illustration of humility is seen in John 13. Jesus and the disciples were to have supper together. The disciples were arguing among themselves about who was the greatest (Luke 22:24). In those days, people ate meals in a reclining position, which meant that a person's head would be about eight inches from someone else's feet. It was common courtesy for everyone's feet to be washed before they reclined for eating. But there was no servant available to wash the disciples' feet. None of the disciples were willing to wash everyone else's feet because they were arguing about who was the greatest. So Jesus took off His outer garment, put a towel around His waist, and washed their feet Himself (John 13:4-5). He taught them an unforgettable lesson. When He finished, He said, in effect, "You're to love one another as I have loved you" (v. 15). How did He show His love for them? Not with emotional attachment. Probably the only emotion He felt was disgust because the disciples were full of selfishness and pride. He showed them His love by meeting their need. Likewise, we should meet the needs of others.

We should meet other people's needs spontaneously and involuntarily. Our love should be like a reflex from a humble heart. That kind of heart will always manifest itself. Having a humble heart doesn't mean walking around in ragged clothes and saying, "I'm a worm." That's a false form of pride; it's the beguiling humility of Colossians 2:18. A truly humble person doesn't articulate his humility.

A humble person acts in service to those in need. He puts others before himself and shows that with love in action. First John 3:17 says, "But whosoever hath this world's good, and seeth his brother have need, and shutteth up his compassions from him, how dwelleth the love of God in him?" A person with the love of God will meet needs. Bibilical love is not an emotion; it is service to someone in need. If you say you are a Christian, yet don't love your brother, then you are a liar. A true Christian has God's love in him.

Love in Action

Let me share with you a letter that I received that talks about love serving people's needs:

Dear Pastor John: Some time ago my husband and I had the opportunity to visit Grace Community Church, and I want to tell you what your church is like from a visitor's point of view. Our church is large, too, and our motto is "The church is where love is." I have never felt more welcome anywhere than I did at Grace Church. The people were terrific. They treated us like royalty. One gentleman gave me an early morning tour of Grace Church. During the break between the first and second services, I talked with another man for a while. He asked me if I would like a tape from that morning's service. I said yes! A few weeks later, I received not just one tape, but the whole series on Jesus' Teaching on Divorce. Many of my friends have listened to that series and had many questions answered for them. I just wanted to let you know how wonderful your congregation is.

That's wonderful, isn't it? I know the people she is talking about. The person who gave her a tour didn't really have the time to do that because he had many other responsibilities. The person who sent her the tapes didn't really have the money to do it, but that's how love acts. Love flows from a humble heart. It seeks the comfort and joy of others, not one's self. That has always been true of Grace Church. I pray that it will always be that way—that we will always have an attitude of selfless love that flows out of a humble heart.

D. Unity

I've always been very concerned about unity. Jesus prays to the Father in John 17:21 that all Christians will be one just as He and the Father are one, so that the world will know He

32

was sent by the Father. Jesus always answers my prayers; I'd like to answer His, wouldn't you? He prayed that we would be unified. John 17:21 basically refers to the unity of believers as a result of salvation. However, Jesus also wants us to have unity in the life and purpose of the church. The apostle Paul told the Ephesians to endeavor "to keep the unity of the Spirit in the bond of peace" (Eph. 4:3). He didn't tell them to generate unity; they already had it. They were to maintain the unity God had already given them.

1. The privation of unity

    Unity is an important part of church life. That's why Satan constantly attacks it. Have you ever noticed how many churches split? Some time ago a woman came to me at a camp, saying, "Please, I have to talk to you." We sat down and talked for a while, and she began by saying, "The church I go to is splitting." I asked, "Why?" She said, "I don't know. We can't figure it out. There's so much division and so many personality clashes that we don't really know anymore why we're splitting. What can I do?" I told her to be a peacemaker and to do anything she could to prevent the split for the sake of the testimony of Jesus Christ. She said, "Some people think it's God's will for the church to split." I told her, "God doesn't ever will for that kind of thing to happen." Then I asked her, "Do you all agree on what the Bible teaches?" She said, "Yes; we all agree with each other on that. It's just that there are many personality conflicts." That is tragic.

2. The preservation of unity

    a) Exemplified

        Some time ago, my wife and I had the opportunity to talk with the daugher of W. A. Criswell, who pastors the First Baptist Church of Dallas. She told us, "Dad once had a man on his church staff who tried to split our church. He was very torn about that. One Sunday he became so concerned about it that he called a construction company and said, "Before next Sunday, I want kneeling benches installed in every pew in this church." By next Sunday, every pew had kneeling benches. (They're still there today.) When everybody came into the church, he said, "By the grace of God, in the last seventy years or so there has never been a split in this church, and there never will

33

be." Then he told the entire congregation to kneel on the kneeling benches in prayer. God healed the rifts that had been developing in the congregation.

Unity brings God glory. It honors His name. I believe that Satan is incessantly trying to divide churches. I thank God and praise Him that Grace Church has never experienced a split. There have been people who wanted to leave because some thing didn't happen the way they wanted it to. Even if they were right, humility and love don't act to bring about division. Everybody should have a desire for unity in the oneness of the Spirit. We should all endeavor to have unity. Satan wants to shred us apart. He always tries to make someone unhappy enough to start a faction.

I'm grateful to God for the sweet unity there is among the staff of Grace Church. We always watch out though, because we know that Satan wants to sow discord. So we always pray and ask God, "Give us a congregation full of peacemakers that want to maintain unity and not sow discord." Even if the person sowing the discord is right over some trivial matter, he should say, "God, You and I know that I'm right, but I'm going to set that aside and seek unity."

b) Exhorted

Nobody is perfect—there are always going to be little things that people disagree about. Nevertheless, we should always get on our knees together and seek to maintain the unity of the Spirit and the bond of peace (Eph. 4:3). That was the desire of the New Testament writers. Paul poured his heart out to the Corinthians and said, "Now I beseech you, brethren, by the name of our Lord Jesus Christ, that ye all speak the same thing, and that there be no divisions among you, but that ye be perfectly joined together in the same mind and in the same judgment. For it hath been declared unto me of you, my brethren, by them who are of the house of Chloe, that there are contentions among you" (1 Cor. 1:10-11). He couldn't stand to see the division among the Corinthians. He adds in verse 13, "Is Christ divided?" In other words, he is saying, "Christ is not divided!" In Philippians 1:27 Paul tells the Philippians that they should be "striving together for the faith of the gospel."

Do you see the attitudes mentioned above in your life? Is your life characterized by obedience? Are you progressing in maturity and becoming more sancitified as you hear the Word and apply it? Do you see yourself growing in such a way that as you get older you will reach the peak of dedication in your spiritual life? Do you have an attitude of humility? Are you meeting other people's needs with loving actions that come from a humble heart? Do you truly seek to make peace and maintain the unity of the Spirit? We should seek all of those things in our lives. That is God's will for us.

Focusing on the Facts

1. Where does the life of a church come from (see p. 23)?
2. What happens when a church is reorganized but the attitudes of its people aren't worked on (see p. 23)?
3. What happens when right spiritual attitudes are present in a church? Why (see pp. 23-24)?
4. What is wrong with merely telling the people of a church how to behave? What should be the emphasis of a minstry (see p. 24)?
5. Define obedience. Why should we live obedient lives (see p. 24)?
6. What often happens when a Christian is confronted about his sin? Give an example (see p. 26).
7. What should be true about older people who have been Christians for many years? Why (see pp. 26-27)?
8. Why do some believers stop serving Christ (see p. 27)?
9. Did God need us to become saved in order for His work to go on? Support your answer (see p. 28).
10. What has God called Christians to? What does a man deny when he follows Christ (Matt. 10:38-39)? According to Philippians 2:3-4, how are Christians to apply humility (see p. 29)?
11. Explain the perspective a Christian should have of himself (see p. 29).
12. Suggest some examples of what a humble Christian will do for another Christian (see pp. 29-30)?
13. Describe the kind of love that exists in the world (see p. 30).
14. What is biblical love? Support your answer (see p. 30).
15. What kind of person can show true biblical love? What kind of person can't? Why (see p. 30)?
16. Who is your neighbor, and how are you to show your love for him (see p. 31)?
17. How should we meet other people's needs? What should our love be like (see p. 31)?
18. Why did Jesus pray to the Father for all Christians to be unified

(John 17:21)? What does Ephesians 4:3 say about the unity of believers (see p. 33)?

19. What does unity among believers do for God? If a believer rightly disagrees with other believers about a trivial matter, what should he do (see p. 34)?

20. What did Paul exhort the Corinthian believers to do, according to 1 Corinthians 1:10-11 (see pp. 34-35)?

Pondering the Principles

1. One of the important spiritual attitudes a Christian must possess is obedience. Read John 14:15, 23. How are we to show our love for God? What will happen to the man who keeps God's commandments? What does Jesus call those who obey His commands (John 15:14)? According to Ephesians 2:10, what were we created to do? Read 1 John 2:3-6. What does verse 4 say about those who do not keep God's commandments? What does verse 5 say about those who do? How are we to walk, according to verse 6? When a person asks Christ to come into his life, he is submitting himself to the lordship of Christ. Examine your life right now and make sure that you are living in total submission to Christ's lordship.

2. God commands Christians to be humble. Read Romans 12:3, 10 and Philippians 2:3-5. How are you to view yourself? How are you to view others? Do you find yourself hoping to receive recognition and praise when you do acts of service in your church? Read Philippians 3:4-9 and Galatians 6:14, and explain what Paul says about pride in those passages.

3. A Christian is to show his love for others through actions. Do you know any people in your church who have needs? Are you willing to take the time to meet any of those needs? Whether you really care about your brothers and sisters in Christ is revealed by how willing you are to meet their needs (James 2:15-17). If you know someone in your church who has a need, then do whatever you can this week to meet that need. Make a habit of meeting other people's needs instead of waiting for others to meet those needs.

4. Unity in a church brings God glory. Do you seek to maintain unity in your church? Are there people in your church you avoid because of personality conflicts? How do you think God feels

about people who are divided over insignificant things? What would unbelievers think if they saw disunity in your church? If you have a grudge against anyone in your church, ask God to give you a forgiving heart. Tell that person that you desire to put aside your grudge and "keep the unity of the Spirit in the bond of peace" (Eph. 4:3).

3
The Anatomy of a Church—
Part 3
(The Internal Systems—Part B)

Outline

Introduction

Review
I. The Skeleton
   A. A High View of God
   B. The Absolute Authority of Scripture
   C. Sound Doctrine
   D. Personal Holiness
   E. Spiritual Authority
II. The Internal Systems
   A. Obedience
   B. Humility
   C. Love
   D. Unity

Lesson
   E. Willingness to Serve
      1. Explained
         a) A look at servants
            (1) Their position
            (2) Their motives
         b) A look at service
            (1) The need for your giftedness
            (2) The nature of your giftedness
      2. Exemplified
         a) By Epaphras
         b) By Epaphroditus
   F. Joy
      1. Defined
      2. Defended

G. Peace
   1.   A contentment in peace
   2.   A commission for peace
   3.   A commitment to peace
H. Thankfulness
   1.   The charge for thankfulness
   2.   The causes for thankfulness

Introduction

In this study *The Anatomy of a Church*, we've divided the human body into four basic elements: the skeleton, the internal systems, the muscles, and the flesh. A body must have all those things. The church, which is the Body of Christ, must also have those elements.

Review

I. THE SKELETON (see pp. 9-17)

A church must have a skeleton, or it will be a shapeless blob. There are certain nonnegotiable, foundational things that form a church's skeleton:

A. A High View of God (see pp. 10-12)

In order for a church to become all that God wants it to be, it must focus on the Lord. It is possible to focus on many other things and forget about focusing on God. When a church focuses on Him, then everything else falls into place. A church cannot compromise its view of God, because the Lord is supreme and everything is to be done for His consummate glory. Whatever you do is to be done for the glory of God (1 Cor. 10:31).

B. The Absolute Authority of Scripture (see pp. 12-13)

We cannot focus on God unless we know who He is, and we cannot know who He is unless we read His revelation of Himself in the Word of God. A church must affirm the absolute authority of Scripture.

C. Sound Doctrine (see pp. 13-14)

A church must learn about God and the basic truths about everything from His Word.

D. Personal Holiness (see pp. 14-15)

Everybody should be applying to their lives the truths they learn from the Bible.

E. Spiritual Authority (see pp. 16-17)

The leaders of a church are to hold people accountable for living the truths they learn from the Word of God.

Those things make up the framework of a church. A church must have a high view of God, which makes it committed to learning about Him in the revelation He has given in His Word. The truths of His Word must be taught in a clear, practical way so that people can apply them to their lives. The application of those truths leads to personal holiness. The people of a church are to submit to those God places in positions of spiritual authority. Since all those elements are to be present in the framework of a church, they must be modeled and preached repeatedly to the people of a church.

II. THE INTERNAL SYSTEMS

A body must have internal organs to give it life. If a body just had a skeleton, muscles, and flesh, it wouldn't really be alive. The same thing is true with a church: There can't just be the affirmation of solid doctrinal foundations; there must be life flowing through. That life comes from proper attitudes. We must battle for our minds to have proper attitudes, "for as [a man] thinketh in his heart, so is he" (Prov. 23:7). The goal of ministry in a church should be to get people to have proper spiritual attitudes. You should learn to cultivate the right kind of thinking so that you may be "renewed in the spirit of your mind" (Eph. 4:23). Paul told the Philippians to think about certain things (Phil. 4:8), so that they would be spiritually minded—that they would have the mind of Christ.

Don't try to control your behavior; try to control your thoughts. When your thoughts are under control, you are able to produce proper behavior. You would be a hypocrite if you tried to produce right actions with wrong motives and attitudes. That's why we emphasize that people have proper spiritual attitudes rather than try to conform their outward behavior. If a person thinks right, he will act right. That's why we're not interested in conforming people to a set of external rules. We're interested in cultivating

41

proper attitudes that honor God and make the church what it should be: a whole, healthy, productive representative of Jesus Christ.

Let's review the attitudes that we've already studied.

A. Obedience (see pp. 24-27)

Obedience is the *sine qua non* of all attitudes. It is an all-pervasive attitude. It mean obeying God at any cost and not compromising. An obedient person does whatever God tells him to do. He doesn't try to justify his sin; rather, he always seeks to do the Lord's will. Internal obedience is better than any external act of worship (1 Sam. 15:22). When a person is obedient, then he will have all the other right spiritual attitudes. If a person is not willing to obey God, then he is going to experience trials and negative circumstances.

B. Humility (see pp. 27-30)

A person with the attitude of humility sees other people as more important than himself. The needs, wants, happiness, joy, and reputation of another person are more important than his own. Humility was expressed by the Lord as selflessness (Phil. 2:5-8). Humility is an essential attitude for the people of a church to have because pride is devastating.

C. Love (see pp. 30-32)

Love is humility in action. Humility and love are inseparable. Only humble people can love. I can't give of myself to you unless I care more about you than I do about myself. I can't abandon myself to your needs unless I am really humble. Humility is the launching pad for love. If humility is selflessness, then love is selfless service.

D. Unity (see pp. 33-35)

When the people of a church are committed to obedience, and act with love because their hearts are humble, then they will have unity. Humility leads to love and love leads to unity. When people meet each other's needs, then they will have the kind of interchange that builds the true one-heart, one-mind, one-soul unity that the Bible speaks of. It's always important to remember that unity comes from humility.

Let's go on now to talk about more attitudes that the people of a church should have.

E. Willingness to Serve

   1. Explained

People have said to me, "We don't come to Grace Church anymore. We've gone to another church where we are needed." It's possible that some of those people were led by God to go to another church. However, some people leave because they think Grace Church has so many people that they're not needed anymore. But if a church has a large number of people, then there are going to be a large number of needs. Some people leave to go to another church because there is a need for someone to run a program. That's all right but serving others isn't necessarily related to church-designed programs. You may say, "I don't sing in the choir, teach a class, or sweep the floor; therefore, I'm not needed. " Look at the people around you in your church. There are all kinds of people with needs!

   a) A look at servants

   (1) Their position

In 1 Corinthians 4:1, Paul says, "Let a man so account of us, as the ministers of Christ." In other words, "When the time comes to render a judgment about my co-workers and me, let it be said that we were servants of Christ."

There are several words in the Greek language for *servant*, and Paul used the one that best conveyed the idea of a lowly servant, (Gk., hupēretēs, "an underrower"). In those days, large wooden three-tiered ships called *triremes* were propelled by slaves chained to their oars in the hull. The slaves on the lowest tier were called "underrowers." Paul and his co-workers did not want to be exalted; they wanted to be known as third-level galley slaves who pulled their oars.

   (2) Their motives

Many people want to be hotshots, but God just wants people who will be obedient servants. In 1 Corinthians 4:2 Paul says, "It is required in stewards, that a man be found faithful." God doesn't want a person to come up with a clever new way to pull his oar and shear off everybody else's oars in the process! He wants faithful rowers who see themselves as willing servants.

In verse 3 Paul continues, "With me it is a very small thing that I should be judged of you, or of man's judgment." He was saying, "I'm not asking for your opinion on my service. I'm not serving you to get praise. I can't accept your judgments about my service to the Lord Jesus Christ."

People can't always tell the motive of a servant. You can do something that appears to be right and be praised for it, even though you did it with corrupt motives. You can do something with pure motives and be cursed for it. Sometimes I'll preach from my heart and the sermon will be terrible, yet some dear person will come to me and say, "That was the greatest sermon you've ever preached." But there have been times when I've preached well from good motives and someone has said, "You didn't seem like yourself today. You seemed to be fumbling around during the sermon." A servant will be criticized, praised, evaluated, blessed, and cursed by people. But Paul didn't let that affect him. He told the Corinthians, "I'm not going to let your judgments bother me. I just want to serve the way I should. I'm not interested in what you think, because you don't understand my motives." He even adds at the end of verse 3, "Yea, I judge not mine own self." In other words, "I can't even trust my own judgment because I'm so biased in my own favor." Then in verse 4 he says "For I know nothing against myself, yet am I not hereby justified; but He that judgeth me is the Lord." Just the mere fact that we're doing something good doesn't justify us. We shouldn't judge anything before the Lord comes and manifests the attitudes and motives of our hearts.

So, God has called us to be third-level galley slaves. We are to be faithful servants. We shouldn't try to make a reputation for ourselves or evaluate ourselves favorably; let the Lord do the judging. We're to serve the Lord "with all humility of mind" (Acts 20:19a). Humility and the willingness to serve are inextricably woven together.

In fact, if you were to cultivate in your life just one of the attitudes that we've discussed so far, the result would be that you would have all the other attitudes present in your life. You wouldn't be able to have love unless you had humility, and you wouldn't be able to have humility unless you had love. You wouldn't be able to have unity with others unless you had love and humility. You can't have a servant's heart unless you have love and humility. All of those attitudes are interwoven. If each of us would concentrate on cultivating at least one of those attitudes, then everything else will find its proper place.

b) A look at service

(1) The need for your giftedness

Service to others doesn't necessarily have to be related to church-designed programs. In Romans 12 Paul talks about the function of servants, using the human body as an analogy: "For as we have many members in one body, and all members have not the same office [function], so we, being many, are one body in Christ, and every one members one of another. Having then gifts differing according to the grace that is given to us, whether prophecy, let us prophesy . . . or ministry, let us wait on our ministering; or he that teacheth, on teaching; or he that exhorteth, on exhortation; he that giveth, let him do it with liberality; he that ruleth, with diligence; he that showeth mercy, with cheerfulness" (vv. 4-8). Paul was saying, "Use the God-given ability you have to minister to others!" You don't need to have a program to be able to minister to others. Let the abilities God has given you flow from your life, whether it be in a structured program or in personal interaction. A believer is indwelt and empowered by the Holy Spirit for the purpose of serving others; so not to serve is to create a bottleneck. Don't go to your church and say, "There are too many people; I don't know where I can serve." If you're filled with the Holy Spirit, God wants to cultivate through you a ministry that is essential for that church.

(2) The nature of your giftedness

Paul mentions in Romans 12:6-8 some categories of ministry: prophecy (preaching), ministry, teaching, exhorting, giving, ruling, and mercy (see also 1 Cor. 12:4-11). Each of those categories is very broad. Within the category of giving, there are many ways to give. Within the category of showing mercy, there are many ways of showing mercy. There are many different styles of preaching and teaching. Each of us is gifted uniquely by the Lord with a different amount of giftedness from each of the categories above. The Lord has given each of us the blend of gifts necessary to enable us to minister the way He wants us to. Looking back on my own life, I can see that God has called me to preach, teach, lead, exhort, and perhaps demonstrate the gift of knowledge. He blends certain gifts in different ways in each one of us so that we're like spiritual snowflakes—no two of us the same. That's why it's important that every one of us serve in the way each is gifted. God doesn't want us to be spectators.

Everyone Is a Minister

A few years ago, *Moody Monthly* magazine published an article about Grace Church. At that time, we were in a smaller building and bursting at the seams with people. After surveying the church and interviewing different people, the writer decided to entitle his article "The Church with Nine Hundred Ministers." He did that because we had nine hundred people at the time, and everyone was actively serving. We didn't have many formal programs then but everybody was ministering his gifts. People were always calling the church and asking if they could visit someone in the hospital, if the nursery needed more helpers, if someone was needed to clean the restrooms and windows, if help was needed to evangelize others, or if someone was needed to teach a class. Everyone made himself available. People would also share with each other how God was blessing their ministry, and they would give God the glory for what was happening. That's the way a church should be.

Sometimes when a church becomes big, people think, *Let other people take care of the needs*. But the bigger a church becomes, the greater the need is for everyone to be serving. Remember too that serving isn't always related to completing specified program goals. Every Christian in the Body of Christ is meant to serve. If you want to be obedient and experience joy and blessing, then use your gifts. Don't worry about not being able to analyze the blend of giftedness God has given you. I don't know exactly how I am gifted; I do know I've been gifted to preach and teach. Don't let a computer analyze your gift. A computer isn't going to know anything about that. The only way I've been able to figure out how God has gifted me is by looking back at what He has done through my life. When you use your giftedness to serve others and allow the power of the Spirit to work through you, then you also will be able to look back at your ministry and see how God is using you.

A Single Area of Ministry

There are always needs to be met. I learned that 70 percent of the people more than eighteen years old in the area around Grace Church are single. Those single people are mainly composed of divorcees, single parents, and swingers. They have needs. The single people at Grace Church have needs, too.

Let me say this to Christians who are single: Don't think that you have to get married. In 1 Corinthians 7, Paul said to get married only if you don't have the gift of singleness (v. 9). If you can stay single, then do it. I believe that single people are a great resource for spiritual ministry because they're not encumbered. In 1 Corinthians 7:32-35, Paul says that single people have more time to serve the Lord than married people, who have to care for the needs of spouse and family. It's not wrong to get married; it's just that if you can be single, then take advantage of your singleness for the sake of ministry.

There are many other areas of ministry a person can get involved in. Cultivate the giftedness that God has given you and become active in whatever ministry God leads your heart to.

2. Exemplified

    a) By Epaphras

        In Colossians 4:12, Paul writes, "Epaphras . . . is one of you, a servant of Christ." Notice that Paul didn't say anything like, "Epaphras, the seminary graduate," or, "Epaphras, the Phi Beta Kappa member with a Ph.D." He just said, "Epaphras, is one of *you*, a servant of Christ." Isn't that beautiful? I used to think it would be wonderful to be able to say on a Christian's tombstone, "One of us, a servant of Christ." Being a servant of Christ is a very high calling.

Paul continued, "[He] greeteth you, always laboring fervently for you in prayers" (v. 12*b*). Was Epaphras a great orator or preacher? No. His ministry was to pray for the Colossians. What was he praying for? He prayed that the Colossians might "stand perfect and complete in all the will of God" (v. 12*c*). Epaphras was burdened for everybody's spiritual development. I believe that he had the gift of faith, because that gift is linked to prayer (Matthew 21:22). I don't know what other categories of giftedness Epaphras had, but he certainly made the most of his gift of faith. He prayed fervently for the Colossians.

b) By Epaphroditus

Paul writes about another man with a true servant's heart in Philippians 2. In verse 25, he says "Epaphroditus, my brother and companion in labor, and fellow soldier, but your messenger . . . ministered to my need." Epaphroditus was a companion to Paul. Do you know how valuable a companion is when you're in a battle defending the gospel? Many people need that kind of support. Paul continued, "He longed after you all, and was full of heaviness, because ye had heard that he had been sick" (v. 26). Epaphroditus's heart was heavy because the Philippians were sad about his being sick. He wasn't concerned about the fact that he was sick; he was distressed because the Philippians were sad that he was sick! The relationship between Epaphroditus and the Philippians must have been a loving one. He wasn't the kind of missionary who writes to his church, "Pray for me; I have a hangnail!" According to verse 27, Epaphroditus "was sick near unto death." Verse 30 says that "for the work of Christ, he was near unto death." He was so busy meeting Paul's needs that he didn't regard his own life.

People like Epaphroditus are going to be noticed in heaven. It's hard to find people like him. Paul says to the Philippians in verse 29, "Receive him . . . and hold such in reputation." Why? Because he was a helper and companion.

A willing servant is spontaneous in what he does. If you have a willingness to serve, your ministry will flow from you. You can either sit back and say, "I don't know if I want to get involved in that; I don't know if I want to work with those people," or just get involved and serve.

F. Joy

   1. Defined

      What is joy? It's an outward exuberance. It's the response of the heart, soul, and mind of a person to his relationship with Jesus Christ.

      There is a seriousness in the Word of God. It is sobering to come before the infinitely holy, all-wise, sovereign God. There is a great seriousness in struggling with the terrible anxieties of life and death and all that our humanness brings upon us. Many things fill us with pain. But at the same time, we are filled with joy. We have a knowledge deep in our souls that all is well and that, ultimately, everything will be glorious.

      When we study the Word of God and obey the Lord, we will experience joy. First John 1:4 says, "These things write we unto you, that your joy may be full." Romans 14:17 says that the kingdom of God is "righteousness, and peace, and joy in the Holy Spirit." Jesus says in John 17:13 that He came to give us joy. Paul said, "Rejoice in the Lord always; and again I say, Rejoice" (Phil. 4:4).

      I'm convinced that joy is linked to a willingness to serve. When people get involved in serving and using the gifts God gave them, then they experience joy. There is joy in giving yourself away. People who are introspective are always trying to meet their own needs and solve their own problems; consequently, they become ingrown, self-contemplating, miserable human beings. It's people who give of themselves who are filled with joy.

   2. Defended

      I don't let things steal my joy. I fight to maintain the joy I have. Some people try to take away my joy. They'll come to me and say, "John, we've got a very serious problem." I'll say, "What is it?" Often the problem will be some insignificant thing. So I'll say, "We'll see if the Lord will solve that problem and do what we can." For the occasions that a big problem is brought to my attention, I have cultivated the ability to say, "That's really exciting! That's terrific!" When I say that, some people look at me as if I were not very bright. Why do I say that? Because if I know about a problem, then I can go to God, and He'll help me solve it. But if I don't know about a problem, then I won't be able to do that. I won't have any trouble if I know about a problem, and I have joy because I know the One who solves problems.

A person can choose to lose his joy. He can look for the manure pile in every meadow if he wants to. It's a choice everyone makes. I choose to be joyful and excited about what God does. With the strength the Holy Spirit has given me, I won't let anyone take away my joy, because the Bible commands that I rejoice always (Phil. 4:4). I tell myself, "Rejoice in the God who redeemed you and loved you in spite of your sin. Rejoice that you are going to heaven someday." I will have problems, but there is coming a day when we'll all be in heaven and everybody will be perfect.

Don't let anybody take away your joy. If you don't have the joy of the Lord, it's because you're looking at things with the wrong perspective. Joy is available to all of us. We can rejoice in anything. Romans 8:28 says, "All things work together for good to them that love God"; therefore, whatever happens in our lives should be a source of joy. The happiest people I've seen are those who have just solved a problem.

G. Peace

That's a beautiful word, isn't it? Jesus said, "Peace I leave with you, my peace I give unto you; not as the world giveth, give I unto you. Let not your heart be troubled, neither let it be afraid" (John 14:27). Jesus gave us His peace. First Corinthians 7:15 says that "God hath called us to peace." Philippians 4:7 says to let the peace of God rule your heart. Second Corinthians 13:11 says to "live in peace." First Thessalonians 5:13 says to "be at peace among yourselves."

1. A contentment in peace

   Whereas joy is an outward exuberance, peace is an inward contentment that senses everything is under control. If there is sin in your life, then you won't experience peace. But when your life is cleansed of sin and you're walking in the Spirit, you'll have peace. We should never allow anyone to take away our peace.

   At Grace Church, we try to cultivate in the hearts of people an attitude of peace, rest, and confidence in God. There is no reason to be troubled. Paul said to "be anxious for nothing" and let the peace of God rule your souls (Phil. 4:6a, 7). All of us experience trials that make us anxious. We don't live in perfect peace, yet we are to have an attitude of peace.

2. A commission for peace

   In Matthew 5:9 our Lord says, "Blessed are the peacemakers; for they shall be called the sons of God." Christians should be peacemakers. You couldn't do anything more wonderful for the kingdom of God and the church of Jesus Christ than to be a peacemaker. Human nature tends toward conflict. Job said, "Yet man is born unto trouble, as the sparks fly upward" (5:7). People continually experience personality conflicts. Yet we are called to be peacemakers. We're to help soothe conflict, not foment it. Sometimes an insignificant problem can be taken out of proportion by people and become a tidal wave. People are more inclined to increase trouble than be a peacemaker. We've all done that.

3. A commitment to peace

   We must have in our hearts a commitment to always say, "I am at peace, God is in control, and I'll be a peacemaker." Every time you get into a conflict, be a peacemaker. When you see two people in a conflict, make them embrace each other in peace. Don't take sides with anyone against another person. Try to find the good in a person instead of focusing on the bad. Cultivate proper relationships and be a peacemaker. Start in your own family. If you know that saying a certain thing will irritate someone, then don't say it. Sometimes when I'm right about something and someone else thinks I'm wrong, I won't assert that I'm right because I don't want to disrupt the peace that's between us. I won't compromise my convictions, but I'm also not going to defend my rights if that means disrupting things. Peace is more important to me than having my own way. However, if someone denies the truth of God, then I will battle for what is right. With the people in the family of God, though, we are to be peacemakers.

H. Thankfulness

First Thessalonians 5:18 says, "In everything give thanks; for this is the will of God in Christ Jesus concerning you." People say, "If only I had a better job," or, "If only I had a better spouse," or, "If only I didn't have problems." However, we're to be thankful.

1. The charge for thankfulness

Giving thanks can be a powerful thing. If you can cultivate a thankful heart, then you will solve many of your problems. Offering thanks and praises to God helps you to stop focusing on your problems. That was true for the psalmist. Whenever a problem developed, he would cry out to the Lord in despair. He would say, "Why are the wicked allowed to prosper?" King David had that attitude when he fled from his son Absalom, who wanted to take over his throne. But eventually he started thinking about all the good things that God had done for him. He started saying things like, "God, You are so mighty and glorious!" An attitude of thankfulness and praise developed. When that happened, his perspective changed; he no longer dwelled on the negative things happening around him. When King David cultivated an attitude of thankfulness in the midst of fleeing from Absalom, he was no longer in despair.

If you are experiencing problems and grumbling all the time, it's not because of your circumstances; it's because of your inability to be thankful for the positive things God has brought into your life. Cultivate an attitude of thankfulness. Let your lips be filled with praise!

2. The causes for thankfulness

There are many things to be thankful for:

a) Psalm 30:4—"Give thanks at the remembrance of his holiness."

b) Psalm 106:1—"Give thanks unto the Lord, for he is good; for his mercy endureth forever."

c) 2 Corinthians 9:15—We are to be thankful for the gift of Christ.

d) Revelation 11:17—We should be thankful for Christ's power and His coming kingdom.

e) 1 Thessalonians 2:13—Be thankful for those who receive and apply the Word of God.

f) Romans 7:23-25—Be thankful that Christ has delivered you from the power of indwelling sin.

g) 1 Corinthians 15:57—Give thanks to God for the fact that He has given us victory over death.

h) Daniel 2:23—Daniel expressed thankfulness to God for the wisdom and strength that was given to him.

i) 2 Corinthians 2:14—We should be thankful for the triumph of the gospel.

j) Romans 6:17—Be thankful for the conversion of people.

k) Romans 1:8—Give thanks to God for people that exhibit their faith.

l) 2 Thessalonians 1:3—We should be thankful when we see believers working hard for the sake of the kingdom and showing love to one another.

m) 1 Corinthians 1:4—Thank God for the grace that He bestows on believers.

n) 2 Corinthians 8:16—Be thankful for those who have a zeal for Christ in their lives.

Don't complain when you're in bad circumstances; cultivate a heart of thankfulness. You may say, "I could be thankful if my circumstances weren't so bad." That's no excuse. If you're not a thankful person, it's because you think you deserve better circumstances than those you currently have. But if you got what you deserved, you'd be in hell. So, don't think you deserve good circumstances. Cultivate a heart of thankfulness for whatever God gives you. That will take all the sourness out of your life.

Thankfulness, peace, joy, a willingness to serve, unity, love, humility, and obedience are all simple attitudes. If you have just one of those attitudes reigning in your life, then you will have all of the others. If you are obedient, then you will naturally have all the other attitudes. If you are humble, then you will love others and bring about unity. If you have that kind of love, then you will want to serve others. Serving others out of love is what gives joy and a deep sense of peace.

When you have that kind of joy and peace, and your life is filled with meaningful service, then you are going to offer thanks to God.

If your life is totally dominated by love, you'll be obedient, because if you love God, you'll obey His commandments (John 14:15). If you love God, you're going to be humble. That humility will bring about unity. Having that kind of love in your life will also motivate you to serve others, which in turn will give you joy, peace, and thanksgiving for the One you love. If you seek unity with other believers, then you'll be loving, humble, and obedient.

Notice that Galatians 5:22-23 says, "The fruit [not 'the fruits'] of the Spirit is love, joy, peace, long-suffering, gentleness, goodness, faith, meekness, self-control." Either all or none of the fruit is present in your life. You can't say, "My life is full of a true love for God that is generated by the Holy Spirit, but I'm miserable and have no joy in my life." A life filled with love is also going to have joy, peace, gentleness, and goodness.

Cultivate in your life just one of the attitudes that we've studied, and the others will be present. Those are the attitudes that change a church, and a church with those kinds of attitudes can change the world.

Focusing on the Facts

1. Why do some people leave a church? Must service always be related to church-designed programs? Explain (see p. 43).
2. Discuss the word *servant* (Gk., *hupēretēs*) that Paul used in 1 Corinthians 4:1 (see p. 43).
3. According to 1 Corinthians 4:2, what is required of a steward (see p. 43)?
4. What was Paul telling the Corinthians in 1 Corinthians 4:3a (see p. 44)?
5. How are we to serve, according to Acts 20:19 (see p. 44)?
6. In Romans 12:4-8, Paul encourages us to use our ability to minister to others. Explain how it is that each of us is uniquely gifted (see p. 46).
7. What is the best way to figure out how God has gifted you (see p. 47)?
8. Why are the single people of a church potentially the greatest resource for spiritual ministry (1 Cor. 7:32-35; see p. 47)?
9. What was Epaphras's ministry to the Colossians? How did Paul describe that ministry (Col. 4:12; see pp. 47-48)?

10. What did Epaphroditus do for Paul (Phil. 2:25)? Why was his heart heavy (v. 26)? What happened to him as a result of the way he ministered to Paul (vv. 27, 30)? As a result, what did Paul command the Philippians to do to Epaphroditus (v. 29); (see pp. 48-49)?
11. A willing servant is _____ in what he does (see p. 49).
12. Define joy. What is joy linked to? What happens to a person who is always focusing on his own needs (see p. 49)?
13. What should be our response to problems? Why (see pp. 49-50)?
14. If you don't have joy, then what is probably the problem? Why should everything be a source of joy, according to Romans 8:28 (see p. 50)?
15. What does Jesus tell us in John 14:27 (see p. 50)?
16. Define peace. How can we experience peace (see p. 51)?
17. What should you do when you see two people in a conflict? Should you always defend yourself if you are right about something and someone else is wrong? Explain (see pp. 51-52).
18. What is the command of 1 Thessalonians 5:18 (see p. 52)?
19. What is wrong with a Christian who has problems and grumbles all the time (see p. 52)?
20. Mention at least five things we should be thankful for (see pp. 52-53).
21. What will happen if you cultivate one of the spiritual attitudes that we've studied? Explain the different ways that can happen (see pp. 53-54).
22. Explain the significance of the singular form of the word *fruit* in Galatians 5:22 (see p. 54).

Pondering the Principles

1. Are you involved in some form of service at your church? What attitudes do you have when you serve? Why do you serve? It is important for you not only to be serving in your church but to have the right attitudes and goals when serving. Would God be able to say that all of your service comes from a loving, humble, and willing heart? Would He be able to say that you serve for the sake of others and for His glory? Think about how God would describe you as a servant. Find your weaknesses and work on them so that you may become a true servant of Christ.

2. Paul commanded that we "rejoice in the Lord always" (Phil. 4:4). Read Psalms 5:11; 28:7; 63:7; 119:111, 162; and Luke 10:20. Explain what caused the people in those verses to be joyful. Read Luke 6:22-23; 2 Corinthians 12:10; James 1:2; and 1 Peter 4:13. Using those verses, explain how we should respond to negative circum-

stances. What are some things God has done for you that give you joy? Do you have joy even in the midst of negative circumstances? Ask God to help you have a joyful perspective in every circumstance, because "all things work together for good to them that love God " (Rom. 8:28).

3. Are you a peacemaker? Look at the conflicts that you've had with other people in the past. How did you handle those situations? Did you make a conscious effort to be a peacemaker? Are there better ways you could have handled those situations? Use your ideas to help you in your future relations with people. If you have children, teach them the importance of being a peacemaker when conflicts arise.

4. According to 1 Thessalonians 5:18, it is God's will that we be thankful in every circumstance. When you pray to God, how much of your prayer time is devoted to focusing on your problems? How much of your prayer time is used to thank God for what He has done in your life? Write a list of the things you can thank God for. Cultivate an attitude of always seeking things to be thankful for. Make a commitment to always devote a part of your prayer time for giving thanks to God.

4

The Anatomy of a Church—
Part 4

(The Internal Systems—Part C)

Outline

Introduction
A. The Church's Failure Discussed
B. The Church's Focus Distorted

Review
 I. The Skeleton
II. The Internal Systems
   A. Obedience
   B. Humility
   C. Love
   D. Unity
   E. Willingness to Serve
   F. Joy
   G. Peace
   H. Thankfulness

Lesson
 I. Self-Discipline
   1. The importance of self-discipline
     a) In competition
       (1) The requirement
       (2) The rules
     b) In combat
       (1) The specifics about battle
       (2) The supplies for battle
         (a) The belt of truthfulness
         (b) The breastplate of righteousness
   2. The implementation of self-discipline
   3. The indifference to self-discipline

Introduction

I was interviewed by the editor of *Discipleship* magazine, and he asked me what my desire for the church is. I told him, "My desire is that it would be what Christ designed it to be." The elders, staff, and congregation of Grace Church all share that desire. That's why it's important for a church to continually reaffirm the basic things that it should be committed to.

A. The Church's Failure Discussed

A few years ago, when I taught a class on ecclesiology at Talbot Theological Seminary, I had my students read Michael Griffiths's book *God's Forgetful Pilgrims* (Grand Rapids: Eerdmans, 1978). In it he said,

> Christians collectively seem to be suffering from a strange amnesia. A high proportion of people who "go to church" have forgotten what it is all for. Week by week they attend services in a special building and go through their particular, time-honoured routine, but give little thought to the purpose of what they are doing.

> The Bible talks about "the bride of Christ" but the church today seems like a ragged Cinderella, hideous among the ashes. She has forgotten that she is supposed to be growing up, as the soap advertisements used to have it, "to be a beautiful lady" (p. 7)!

He's right. The church (especially here in America), which is supposed to be the bride of Christ, is a ragged Cinderella. It needs to reaffirm the nonnegotiable, essential elements that God designed for it to be committed to. That's the intent of this study on The Anatomy of a Church: to study those basic principles.

B. The Church's Focus Distorted

We must be sure that the church doesn't get committed to the wrong principles. Gene Getz, in his book *The Measure of a Church* (Glendale, Calif.: Gospel Light, 1975), said that happens frequently. He wrote:

> Some say a mature church is an active church! They evaluate progress by the number of meetings held each week and by the number of different kinds of programs going on.
>
> Some say a mature church is a growing church! As long as new people are coming and staying, they believe they are a maturing church. As long as the pastoral staff is enlarging, they believe "all is well."
>
> Some say a mature church is a giving church! As long as people are contributing financially to the ongoing program of the church and supporting its many ventures, they believe it is a maturing church.
>
> Some say a mature church is a soul-winning church! They say this is proof positive. When people are bringing others to Christ regularly, when we can account for regular professions of faith and regular baptisms, then for sure we have a New Testament church.
>
> Some say a mature church is a missionary-minded church—a church that supports missions around the world, designating a large percentage of its overall budget to world evangelism.
>
> Some say a mature church is a smooth-running church—a church whose organizational machinery is oiled with every degree of regularity. It is a finely tuned machine with job descriptions, eight-hour days, coffee breaks and punch cards. Everybody does what he was hired to do— on time and efficiently.
>
> Still others say a mature church is a "Spirit-filled" church. This is the church that is enthusiastic and dynamic. It has

lots of emotion and excitement. Everyone in it knows what his gifts are and uses them regularly.

And finally, some say the ultimate mark of maturity is the big church, with thousands coming to Sunday School and church every Sunday. Maturity, to them, is represented by a large paid staff, scores of buses that pick up children every week, multiple programs, a radio and television ministry, a Christian day school, a Christian college and seminary; and oh, yes, a printing press to prepare its own literature.

Unfortunately, some people really believe that what I have stated are biblical marks of maturity (pp. 16-17).

There's nothing wrong with active, growing, giving, soul-winning, missionary-minded, smooth running, big churches. But a cult can have all of those characteristics, too. (It wouldn't be Spirit-filled, though.) None of those things are the heart of the church. That's why we have to look behind the external things of a church and look into its anatomy. We need to know the internal elements of the church. Sometimes pastors visit Grace Church and want to copy the external things that they see going on. But we tell them that the internal things are more important. We're supposed to focus on attitudes, not activities.

Review

I. THE SKELETON (see pp. 9-17)

II. THE INTERNAL SYSTEMS

A body has to have things within it that give it life. The church must have the same. The people of a church must have certain attitudes. A church can't just have external routines.

God chastised the people of Israel when their religion became mere external routine. Through the prophet Amos, He said, "I hate, I despise your feast days, and I will not take delight in your solemn assemblies. Though ye offer me burnt offerings and your meal offerings, I will not accept them; neither will I regard the peace offerings of your fat beasts. Take away from me the noise of thy songs; for I will not hear the melody of thine harps. But let justice run down like waters, and righteousness like a mighty stream" (Amos 5:21-24).

Through Hosea, God said, "O Judah, what shall I do unto thee? For your goodness is like a morning cloud, and like the early dew it goeth away. Therefore have I hewed them by the prophets; I have slain them by the words of my mouth; and thy judgments are as the light that goeth forth. For I desired mercy, and not sacrifice, and his knowledge of God more than burnt offerings" (Hosea 6:4-6). In Isaiah 1:11-15, God told the people of Israel, "To what purpose is the multitude of your sacrifices unto me? saith the Lord; I am full of the burnt offerings of rams, and the fat of fed beasts, and I delight not in the blood of bullocks, or of lambs, or of he-goats. When ye come to appear before me, who hath required this at your hand, to tread my courts? Bring no more vain oblations; incense is an abomination unto me; the new moons and sabbaths, the calling of assemblies, I cannot bear; it is iniquity, even the solemn meeting. Your new moons and your appointed feasts my soul hateth; they are a trouble unto me; I am weary of bearing them. And when ye spread forth your hands, I will hide mine eyes from you; yea, when ye make many prayers, I will not hear." The people of Israel were guilty of external religiosity—they didn't have the right internal attitudes.

I believe that the heart and soul of a ministry should be to lay a skeletal foundation and then spend time trying to create right heart attitudes in people. That's what makes the church a beautiful lady; that's what builds the church up to the fullness of the stature of Jesus Christ.

We've already looked at several of the internal attitudes that should be present in a church:

A. Obedience (see pp. 24-27)

B. Humility (see pp. 27-30)

C. Love (see pp. 30-32)

D. Unity (see pp. 33-35)

E. Willingness to Serve (see pp. 42-49)

F. Joy (see pp. 49-50)

G. Peace (see pp. 50-52)

H. Thankfulness (see pp. 52-54)

Lesson

I. Self-Discipline

   1. The importance of self-discipline

Christians need to realize how important it is for us to conform to God's divine standard. Self-discipline means staying away from sin and doing only those things that are right. That's a simple, clear definition of self-discipline. The disciplined person understands the law of God and doesn't do anything outside the bounds of that standard.

     a) In competition

        (1) The requirement

Paul talks about self-discipline in 1 Corinthians 9:24-27. There, he uses a metaphor that is familiar to all of us to illustrate his point: a race. Beginning in verse 24, he says, "Know ye not that they who run in a race run all, but one receiveth the prize? So run, that ye may obtain." Everyone in a race runs to win the prize; that's why each is in the race. As believers, we have been called to race (Gal. 5:7; Phil. 2:16; Heb. 12:1-2). We are to run to win. What is necessary to accomplish that goal? Paul tells us in verse 25: "And every man that striveth for the mastery [competes in athletics] is temperate in all things." In other words, if a person wants to experience victory, he has to be self-disciplined. A man can't win a race if he is thirty pounds overweight. Tremendous discipline is required to keep in shape.

The number of hours an athlete must train so that he can win in competition is staggering. An athlete who competes internationally trains several hours a day for as long as five to ten years of his life. He must push himself to the point where he will not experience pain, to a point beyond a second wind. There is a euphoria beyond pain that only athletes can experience. I've been involved in athletics enough to have experienced that myself. That euphoria is like an incredible sense of freedom and energy, and it only comes beyond pain. It's hard to explain.

(2) The rules

Paul told the Corinthians, "I'm running in a spiritual race. In order to win, I've got to get myself under control." That's what he says in verse 26: "I, therefore, so run, not as uncertainly." In other words, he's saying that he makes sure he stays on course. In 2 Timothy 2:5, Paul tells Timothy that for an athlete to win the crown in a race, he must "strive lawfully" [Gk., *nominōs*]. He must obey the rules of the game. He can't go out of bounds. If he wants to win, he must conform to the rules. That's what Paul told the Corinthians: "I want to win, so I must give my best effort." The Greek verb used for "striveth for the mastery" in 1 Corinthians 9:25 speaks of self-discipline, which includes the idea of staying within the rules.

In verse 27, Paul adds, "I keep under my body, and bring it into subjection, lest that by any means, when I have preached to others, I myself should be a castaway [i.e., be disqualified because of sin]." He didn't want to sin and lose the chance for a spiritual victory any more than an athlete would want to do anything that would cause him to lose a physical victory.

b) In combat

(1) The specifics about the battle

I once had the opportunity to teach a Bible study for the Miami Dolphins football team before a game they played against the Los Angeles Raiders. I taught them from Ephesians 6. Some of them already had their legs and ankles taped, ready for battle. I told them that they had spent a tremendous number of hours and much energy to reach the peak of athletic performance that they were at. Soon, they were going to put on their armor, so to speak, to do battle for a corruptible crown (1 Cor. 9:25). I told them that there was another warfare more important than that: the spiritual warfare for an incorruptible crown—an eternal inheritance that "fadeth not away" (1 Pet. 1:4). For that kind of warfare, there is an armor more important than shoulder pads, chest pads, hip pads, helmets, and all the other things football players wear. It is vital to wear that armor if one is going to know victory in spiritual warfare. I shared with them Ephesians 6:11: "Put on the whole armor of God, that ye may be able to stand against the wiles of the devil." Then I said, "Fighting unprepared against the enemies of your soul would be like fighting the Raiders in your gym shorts, 'for we wrestle not against flesh and blood, but against principalities, against powers, against the rulers of the darkness of this world, against spiritual wickedness in high places'" (Eph. 6:12). We are in a battle, and the battle isn't against other men. Men are only the playthings of the unseen demonic world. The real battle is against demons.

Experiencing the Battle Against Demonic Forces

I will never forget a battle with a demon-possessed girl one night at church. She was kicking, screaming, and throwing furniture. When I walked into the room she said, "Don't let him in!" but the voice that said that wasn't her own. At first that was frightening, and my human response was, "Fine! I'm leaving!" But I began to realize that if the demons didn't like me, then I was on God's team fighting against them. In the power of God, several of us spent hours there until she confessed her sin. God, in his grace, purified her. Since that encounter, I've never doubted that man's battle is against demons. It's a spiritual battle, where men are pawns in the hands of demons.

It's important for us to understand the seriousness of the spiritual warfare wrought against Christ and all who belong to Him. We need to put on "the whole armor of God, that ye may be able . . . to stand" (Eph. 6:13). We have to be prepared for battle.

(2) The supplies for the battle

There are two elements of that armor I'd like to emphasize. They are mentioned in Ephesians 6:14:

(a) The belt of truthfulness

Paul tells us to "stand, therefore, having your loins girded about with truth." There Paul

64

envisions a Roman soldier preparing for battle. If a Roman soldier were to go into battle without a belt, his tunic would fly loosely around him. In hand-to-hand combat, a loose tunic could interfere with a soldier's moves and cause his death. It also made him vulnerable to being grabbed by an enemy soldier. To prevent that from happening, a Roman soldier put on a belt to gather his tunic tightly around him. Paul called it the belt of truthfulness. He associated it with a sincere commitment to self-discipline. We need to be committed to walking the narrow path that God has called us to walk. That isn't easy; there are little voices all along that path calling us away from it. If we love pleasure more than we love God, then we'll divert from the path of self-discipline that God has called us to and enter into sin. The apostle Paul warned that we must be serious about the war we are in and tighten our belts in an act of real commitment to victory.

(b) The breastplate of righteousness

Roman soldiers wore a breastplate over their chests to keep their vital organs from being vulnerable to arrows and knives. Paul called it the breastplate of righteousness (or holiness). We need to live righteous lives—to obey God's laws—or we'll be vulnerable in battle. If we're going to win the race we're in, we've got to discipline ourselves to live pure lives in obedience to God's will. In 2 Corinthians 7:1, Paul says, "Having, therefore, these promises, dearly beloved, let us cleanse ourselves from all filthiness of the flesh and spirit, perfecting holiness in the fear of God." Because we are the sons and daughters of God (2 Cor. 6:18), we've got to be serious about being self-disciplined and living righteously. We need to put on our belts and breastplates and run the race to win. We're to run that race wholeheartedly and stay within the limits of the rules.

2. The implementation of self-discipline

I grieve when I see undisciplined Christians. They're aware of the fact that they're to be obedient, but they're not committed to that command. In Philippians 4:8, Paul commands us, "Finally, brethren, whatever things are true, whatever things are honest, whatever things are just whatever things are pure, whatever things are lovely, whatever things are of good report; if there be any virtue, and if there be any praise, think on these things." Self-discipline is related to our minds. Proverbs 23:7 says, "For as [a man] thinketh in his heart, so is he." A pure, self-disciplined life comes from being saturated with the Word of God. The reason it's important to be taught the Word of God is so that when you become tempted to sin, the Spirit of God can help you to remember God's Word. Reading and meditating on the Scripture is necessary to make the Word reside in your heart. The psalmist said, "Thy word have I hidden in mine heart, that I might not sin against thee" (Ps. 119:11). Your thinking must be controlled with the Word of God. Colossians 3:16 says to "let the word of Christ dwell in you richly." God's Word is the source of discipline, and you must be committed to knowing it.

3. The indifference to self-discipline

I'm concerned about the fact that many Christians today are not self-disciplined. Although God's standards have not changed since He first established them, Christians have widened the narrow path they are called to walk and become tolerant of things that are wrong.

a) Exemplified by adolescents

The pastor of the junior-high school department at our church once shared with me some astounding things. He did a survey at a camp for junior-high-school students and learned that forty-five out of fifty-four had already seen an R-rated movie. Out of thirty-five seventh-grade boys, twenty-five had already seen R-rated movies, and twenty-six had read pornographic magazines. Twenty-four of those seventh graders also went to Christian schools! Many of them watch cable television programs that are filthy.

I was distressed to hear that. A seventh-grade child can't be exposed to an R-rated movie without its having a negative effect on him. He isn't going to easily forget eighteen-foot high images of naked people. Junior-high-school students can't handle that. If you allow your junior-high-age children to go to an R-rated movie, then you're contributing to any sinful responses they may have to the movie and are allowing them to be exposed to things they can't handle. If you allow your children to watch filthy things on cable television, then don't be shocked if someday they don't have any interest in God.

It grieves me that adolescents are being exposed to such things. That doesn't help a teenager who is struggling to learn his identity and develop proper sexual ideas. I'm not being legalistic when I say that; I'm concerned about teenagers being exposed to sin. There is nothing worse the world can do than to display its filth before young eyes.

b) Exemplified by adults

   (1) Parental responsibility

      Those of you who are parents need to set an example for your children. Don't think that they can handle R-rated movies if you go along with them. You are to be good stewards of the children God has given you. If you allow your children to be exposed to things they shouldn't see, then you're going to be accountable for that.

      You may say, "I can't help it if my child sees R-rated movies and looks at pornographic magazines," or, "There's nothing wrong with going to a movie that has profanity if it's a 'good' movie." Saying that only lowers God's standard. The same thing has happened with music. Music today has attacked God's standards to the point where our commitment to purity is broken down. We must be cautious of being subliminally induced to lower the standards God has given us.

   (2) Personal responsibility

      If you attend an R-rated movie, you will contribute to your own sinfulness. Some people say such movies are art, but that's not true. Those who promote R-rated movies say that they have some social value and that they comment on our culture. But that's how they attract good, moral people to see them. Those kinds of movies only devastate people's thoughts. There's no place in a Christian's life for the profanity in PG-rated motives and the nudity in R-rated movies. Don't be victimized by the advertising techniques used to lure you to such films. I feel strongly that a person who looks at massive, incessant images of vile things or looks through pornographic magazines can't expect himself to cultivate godly thinking.

I don't allow myself to be exposed to worldly things because I want to have God's perspective on things, not the world's. That requires being isolated from worldly things. You may say, "But if you isolate yourself like that, then you won't know what's going on." That doesn't bother me. I've never been to an R-rated movie and don't intend to go to one. Nor am I interested in PG movies that will expose my mind to the garbage of the world.

Beloved, we live in a time when disciplined living is important. Don't give in to the cries of the world that say, "Come over here; we'll give you pleasure." If you involve yourself in filthy films or sinful activities, then you have not yet given your life fully to the commitment that God calls for. You've abandoned the path of obedience. We are not to say to ourselves, "Oh, doing that won't be so bad." Paul commands us in Philippians 4:8 to think about things that are good, not things that don't seem bad.

J. Accountability

1. The principle

It is essential to teach everybody in a church that they be accountable to one another. We should be concerned about each other, not what color the carpeting or wallpaper is. People are more important than programs. Let me share with you an example of accountability from Matthew 7: "And why beholdest thou the mote that is in thy brother's eye, but considerest not the beam that is in thine own eye?" (v. 3). In other words, "Why are you more concerned about the little problem in your brother's life than the bigger problem you have in your own life?" Verse 4 continues, "Or how wilt thou say to thy brother,

Let me pull the mote out of thine eye; and, behold, a beam is in thine own eye?" Matthew uses hyperbole here; he's making an exaggerated illustration. But his point is clear: How can you help your brother with his little problem when your own life has a bigger problem?

The principle in those verses is this: We have a responsibility to take care of those things that are in each other's eyes. We have to deal with sin in each other, but before we can do that, we must deal with our own sin (v. 5). Accountability among the people of a church is an important thing. In a relationship of accountability, a person is not just responsible for taking care of others; he is also responsible for making sure his own life is right before he tries to do that.

2. The practice

Let's look at a practical application of accountability. Suppose someone that you know at your church stopped coming. It is your responsibility to go to that person and say, "You're forsaking the assembly (Heb. 10:25). You need to be more committed to fellowshiping with God's people." You may say, "Who am I to say that? I've got problems in my own life." Then clean up your life—get the beam out of your eye—so that you can confront that other person's sin. Accountability requires us to be pure. If I become concerned about another person's sin, then I have to become concerned about my own sin, too, or I won't be able to deal with that other person.

Galatians 6:1 says, "Brethren, if a man be overtaken in a fault, ye who are spiritual restore such an one." It takes a person walking in obedience to help a person who is living in disobedience. Before a person can help soneone who is being disobedient, he must have his own life right. Having everyone in a church be accountable to one another has a self-purifying effect on everyone. A church where people are not taught to care about each other will be a church where people are not challenged to cleanse sin from their own lives. Accountability is important. When I'm accountable to you, I become accountable to myself.

a) The approach explained

After we've taken care of the beam in our own eyes, how do we approach the person that has fallen into sin? Matthew 18:15 tells us what do to: "If thy brother

69

shall trespass against thee, go and tell him his fault between thee and him alone." If a person in your church sins, then approach him about it alone. For example, if you know a Christian who is a dishonest businessman and mistreats his employees, then you have an obligation before God to go to that person and—in a loving way—say, "What you are doing is wrong." You may say, "I can't do that. I've got my own problems." Then take care of the problems in your own life! You say, "That will take a while." No; all you need to do is make a prayer of confession (1 John 1:9). Then, with a pure heart and loving spirit, you can approach a Christian who is sinning.

Some other examples of when you should confront other people are if you know someone who is not being faithful to his spouse, parents who aren't bringing up their children as they should, or children who aren't obeying their parents. Knowing that your own life has to be right before you can approach a sinning brother will have a self-purifying effect. Everyone in a church must be accountable to someone else—it doesn't matter who you are. In Galatians 2:11-14, Paul says that he rebuked Peter publicly for doing something wrong. Elders and leaders are not exempt from rebuke. If they are rebuked, it is to be done before the church so that others may fear and avoid sin (1 Tim. 5:20).

b) The appreciation expressed

I once received a letter from someone who had noticed something wrong in my life, and I wrote back to him asking for his forgiveness and thanking him for bringing it to my attention. If something is wrong in my life, I want to know it. But if someone doesn't tell me because they're afraid to, then I'll keep making the same mistake. Everyone in a church should have that kind of accountablility to one another so that everyone's life is pure. Even husbands and wives should hold one another accountable. It isn't right for anyone's sinfulness to be tolerated. Anyone in sin should be lovingly confronted.

c) The antagonism encountered

You say, "What if the sinning person doesn't listen to me?" Matthew 18:16 says, "But if he will not hear thee, then take with thee one or two more, that in the mouth of two or three witnesses every word may be established." If the person you are confronting still doesn't listen, then verse 17 says to "tell it unto the church." Have everyone in the church encourage the sinning brother to repent. That's the responsibility involved in accountability. Doing that helps keep the church pure.

d) The apprehension eliminated

(1) The fear of confronting others

When a church discipline was first applied at Grace Church, a couple of the pastors said to me, "It won't work. The church will be wrecked. You can't have everyone watching out for other people's sins." I said, "The Bible says we're supposed to be accountable to one another. Let's just do it and see what God does." We are not to worry about building the church; Christ said He would take care of that (Matt. 16:18). All we are supposed to do is make sure that everyone in the church understands the Word of God and applies it. The Lord will take care of everything else.

(2) The fruit of confronting others

I have a wonderful illustration of how church discipline worked for the good of Grace Church. A woman called me one day and said, "My husband just left me; he is going to live with another woman." I asked her for the name of that other woman, and she gave it to me. I found the woman's telephone number and called her. The husband of the woman who had called me answered the telephone. I said, "This is John calling from Grace Church. I'm calling in the name of Christ for you to move out of that woman's place before you sin against God, your wife, and your church." He was shocked and said he would go back to his wife. The next Sunday, he came up to me, embraced me, and said, "Thank you! I didn't want to be there. I was tempted, and I thought no one would care about that." He wasn't alienated by my rebuke; rather, he was brought back to the fellowship.

Confrontation is necessary to help restore a sinning brother. Sometimes a Christian will do something he doesn't want to do, and it will require the rebuke of another Christian to pull him out of it. Paul said he struggled with the flesh: "For that which I do I understand not; for what I would, that do I not; but what I hate, that do I" (Rom. 7:15). Confrontation is not intended for invading people's privacy; it's for the purpose of helping others in their battle with sin. We need to be concerned about accountability. That's one reason that Communion is important. It reminds us to make sure our lives are right so that we can restore each other in love and provoke one another to love and good works (Heb. 10:24).

Accountability involves the one-anothers of Scripture. We are to exhort one another (Heb. 10:24-25), pray for one another (James 5:16), love one another (Gal. 5:13; Eph. 4:2; 1 Pet. 1:22), teach one another (Col. 3:16), edify one another (Rom. 14:19; 1 Thess. 5:11), and admonish one another (Rom. 15:14; Col. 3:16). Those things make up the life of the church.

K. Forgiveness

The church can't survive without forgiveness. It's an important attitude because we're human and we all sin. If you can't forgive someone who sins, particularly someone who sins against you, then there is a cancer in you and in the Body of Christ.

1. Clarified

   a) Receiving forgiveness

   Look at what Matthew 6:12 says about forgiveness: "Forgive us our debts [every sin is a debt owed to God and can only be paid by the perfect sacrifice of Christ], as we forgive our debtors." In other words, "God, forgive us as we forgive others." Verses 14-15 tell us, "For if ye forgive men their trespasses, your heavenly Father will also forgive you; but if ye forgive not men their trespasses, neither will your Father forgive your trespasses." If you don't forgive other people, God won't forgive you.

   Matthew 6:14-15 is not talking about the eternal, redemptive forgiveness we receive when we accept Christ as our Savior. It's talking about a parental, temporal forgiveness. It's a forgiveness related to current sin. We need to have a forgiving attitude if we want to have pure, blessed fellowship with God and our brothers and sisters in Christ.

b) Refusing forgiveness

I believe that an unforgiving heart can cause tragedy. I think that the body catches the soul's diseases and that there may be many people who have died because they had an unforgiving spirit. Guilt is the severest of the soul's diseases. Both guilt and an unforgiving heart create bitter feelings.

If you want to be forgiven by the Lord on a daily basis and maintain a pure, sweet fellowship with Him, then you need to have a forgiving heart toward others. How can you possibly not forgive others? Who are you not to forgive? In Matthew 18:23-34 there is a parable about a man that owed his master 10,000 talents (an incalculable debt). The master forgave that man and erased his debt. Later on, that man found a friend who owed him a hundred denarii (a trivial amount compared to the former debt). He strangled him and had him put in jail. At the end of the parable, Jesus said, "How can those of you that have been forgiven an unpayable debt not forgive someone else that wrongs you?"

2. Commanded

Ephesians 4:32 says, "And be ye kind one to another, tenderhearted, forgiving one another, even as God, for Christ's sake, hath forgiven you." We should forgive one another because God has forgiven us. How can we be forgiven so much and forgive others so little? The church needs to be filled with forgiving people, because there will always be people that fail. People are always going to do things that will irritate others or cause problems. If you're willing to forgive an offender, then you'll be free from the bondage of bitterness. You'll also be free to be forgiven by God and experience blessing from Him. Forgiveness is a beautiful attitude. You don't need to have an unforgiving, bitter heart.

When the attitude of forgiveness is not present in a church, there will be problems. By the way, only humble people forgive. A proud person who is sinned against will say, "You can't get away with doing that to someone like me!" But a

73

humble person will say, "You're more important than I am. I want to love you by showing forgiveness."

So, the people of a church must have the attitudes of self-discipline, accountability for others, and forgiveness.

Focusing on the Facts

1. In his book *God's Forgetful Pilgrims*, what did Michael Griffiths say was the problem with many people who go to church (see p. 58)?
2. Gene Getz mentioned some things that people say make a mature church. What are they? Do those characteristics make a mature church? Explain (see pp. 59-60).
3. Define self-discipline (see p. 62).
4. God has called believers to run a race (Gal. 5:7; Phil. 2:16; Heb. 12:1-2). How are we to race (1 Cor. 9:25a)? How can we accomplish that goal (see p. 62)?
5. According to 2 Timothy 2:5, what else must a believer do when he races? What does the Greek verb used for "striveth for the mastery" speak of (1 Cor. 9:25a; see p. 63)?
6. According to Ephesians 6:12, why is it important for us to wear the armor of God in spiritual warfare? Who are our real enemies in spiritual warfare (see p. 64)?
7. What does it mean to put on the belt of truthfulness (see pp. 64-65)?
8. What is meant by putting on the breastplate of righteousness (see p. 65)?
9. What is self-discipline related to? How does a person develop a pure, self-disciplined life? According to Psalm 119:11, what did the psalmist do and why (see p. 66)?
10. If you allow your children to go to an R-rated movie, what are you contributing to in their lives (see pp. 66-67)?
11. A person who watches R-rated movies or reads pornographic magazines can't expect himself to cultivate _____ (see p. 68).
12. What principle is stated in Matthew 7:3-4? What are the two responsibilities of a person in an accountability relationship (see pp. 68-69)?
13. What must you do before you approach a sinning believer (see p. 69)?
14. How are you to approach a sinning believer (Matt. 18:15; see pp. 69-70)?
15. Is anyone exempt from rebuke? Explain (see p. 70).
16. What should you do if a sinning believer doesn't listen to you (Matt. 18:16)? If a sinning believer continues in his sin, what is the church to do (see pp. 70-71)?

17. What is the intent of confronting a sinning believer (see p. 72)?
18. What does Matthew 6:14-15 say about forgiveness (see pp. 72-73)?
19. What can result from one's having an unforgiving heart (see p. 73)?
20. Why should we be willing to forgive one another (Eph. 4:32; see p. 73)? What results from being willing to forgive someone who sins against you (see p. 73)?

Pondering the Principles

1. Living for God is like running a race: it needs to be done with self-discipline, a whole heart, and by keeping the rules. Hebrews 12:1 says, "Therefore, since we have so great a cloud of witnesses surrounding us, let us also lay aside every encumbrance, and the sin which so easily entangles us, and let us run with endurance the race that is set before us" (NASB*). When we live for God, we are to "lay aside every encumbrance." Are there things in your life that divert your attention from God or dampen your enthusiasm for spiritual things? What are they? How are they affecting you? Are you willing to lay those encumbrances aside? Why or why not? Your answers to the last two questions will show how committed you are to God's calling. Read Hebrews 12:1-2 again, and prayerfully make a commitment to "run with endurance the race that is set before us."

2. All believers should be accountable to one another. Having everyone in a church accountable to one another helps keep a church pure. If a coach told an athlete to exercise for four hours every day but wasn't present to make sure the exercises were done, how well do you think the athlete would perform his task? Suppose the athlete is doing one of his exercises wrong and is hurting his chances of performing well in his sport. Should the coach tell the athlete what he's doing wrong? If the coach corrects the athlete's problem, what should be the athlete's response? Have you anyone to be accountable to for what you learn from the Bible? How do you respond when people point out your sins? If you do not have someone to coach you in your walk with God, develop an accountability relationship with someone. If you are already accountable to someone, make sure that neither of you has fallen below the standards God has set for holy living.

3. When someone sins against you, do you think of avenging yourself? How long do you hold grudges against someone who

New American Standard Bible.

75

has offended you? Is it right for you to seek revenge or hold grudges? Why? When someone sins against you, how long does it take you to forgive them? Work on developing a forgiving heart toward others, and make a goal of being able to fogive others immediately when they sin against you.

5
The Anatomy of a Church—
Part 5
(The Internal Systems—Part D)

Outline

Introduction
A. The Vision Described
B. The Vision Discussed

Review
 I. The Skeleton
 II. The Internal Systems
   A. Obedience
   B. Humility
   C. Love
   D. Unity
   E. Willingness to Serve
   F. Joy
   G. Peace
   H. Thankfulness
   I. Self-Discipline
   J. Accountability
   K. Forgiveness

Lesson
   L. Dependence
     1. Running ahead of God
       a) The danger of being presumptuous
       b) The demand for being prayerful
     2. Running with God
       a) An example of dependency
         (1) The panic
         (2) The promise
           (*a*) Expressed
           (*b*) Explained

Introduction

A. The Vision Described

In Revelation 1 is a powerful, wonderful presentation of the Worthy Lamb, the Son of God: "I, John, who also am your brother, and companion in tribulation, and in the kingdom and patience of Jesus Christ, was in the isle that is called Patmos, for the word of God, and for the testimony of Jesus Christ. I was in the Spirit on the Lord's day, and heard behind me a great voice, as of a trumpet, saying, I am Alpha and Omega, the first and the last; and, What thou seest, write in a book, and send it unto the seven churches which are in Asia: unto Ephesus, and unto Smyrna, and unto Pergamum, and unto Thyatira, and unto Sardis, and unto Philadelphia, and unto Laodicea. And I turned to see the voice that spoke with me. And being turned, I saw seven golden lampstands, and in the midst of the seven lampstands one like the Son of man, clothed with a garment down to the foot, and girded about the breasts with a golden girdle. His head and his hair were white like wool, as white as snow; and his eyes were like a flame of fire; and his feet like fine bronze, as if they burned in a furnace; and his voice like the sound of many waters. And he had in his right hand seven stars; and out of his mouth went a sharp two-edged sword; and his countenance was as the sun shineth in its strength" (vv. 9- 16).

B.   The Vision Discussed

John had an incredible vision, and in it he saw the Lord Jesus Christ, the Alpha and the Omega. In that vision, Christ was moving among seven golden lampstands. They represent the seven churches mentioned in verse 11. The seven stars in Christ's hand represent the seven ministers of those churches, according to verse 20. The seven churches of Asia Minor mentioned in verse 11 and described in Revelation chapters 2 and 3 are representative of the different kinds of churches that have existed throughout church history. In the vision John described, we see the Lord moving among His churches, caring for those He purchased with His precious blood. Christ is still actively caring for His church today. John's vision was not a vision just for that place and time; it was a vision for churches everywhere throughout history.

Verse 13 describes Christ as being "clothed with a garment down to the foot" and arrayed with a golden girdle. The prophets, priests, and kings of Israel dressed like that. Isn't it fitting that Christ indeed King, Prophet, and Priest? He is sovereign. He moves in His church as One who speaks from God and takes His people to Him. In verse 14, we read that "His head and his hair were white like wool, as white as snow." That indicates His absolute, pure holiness. Verse 14 also says that "his eyes were like a flame of fire." As Christ moves in His church, He looks at it with a penetrating gaze. His eyes are searching out strengths and weaknesses and looking beyond the surface of things to ascertain what is really going on in His church.

How marvelous it is to know that Christ is alive in His church! It's wonderful to know that the church is not built and maintained by men. Christ is working in the church, and He knows what needs to be done. He searches His church with a penetrating gaze. Verse 15 says that His feet are like fine bronze, as if they blazed in a furnace, and that His voice is like the sound of many waters. Those represent His feet and voice of judgment. When He sees something in the church that displeases Him, He comes and speaks in judgment.

You say, "Why are you reading that?" Because I think it's good to remember that we are a part of the church that Christ is building. We are the lampstand that Christ is caring for. We are the light that Christ is trimming. He is looking at us with a penetrating gaze. He seeks things in us that are not right and brings against them the thunder of His voice in chastening judgment. He seeks to refine us, and if we resist, He will remove His blessing. In the letters to the churches of Asia Minor in Revelation chapters 2 and 3, He commended a few churches but condemned most of them. the Lord did not see in them the purity He sought to find.

Just as Christ moved through the seven churches in Revelation 1:11, He moves through Grace Church. I believe He commends certain things and condemns others; He blesses things that are according to His will and chastens things that are not. It is my prayer that I will be able to stand in behalf of Christ and tell you what His searching eyes want to see in the church. I'm not saying that I'm an anointed prophet of God; I just believe that the Spirit of God has prompted us to study the things that a church should possess.

Review

I. THE SKELETON (see pp. 9-17)

II. THE INTERNAL SYSTEMS

Just as a body is dependent on vital organs to keep it alive, a church is dependent upon certain spiritual attitudes to give it life:

A. Obedience (see pp. 24-27)

B. Humility (see pp. 27-30)

C. Love (see pp. 30-32)

D. Unity (see pp. 33-35)

E. Willingness to Serve (see pp. 42-49)

F. Joy (see pp. 49-50)

G. Peace (see pp. 50-52)

H. Thankfulness (see pp. 52-54)

I. Self-Discipline (see pp. 61-68)

J. Accountability (see pp. 68-72)

K. Forgiveness (see pp. 72-74)

All those attitudes must be cultivated in God's people. I believe the Lord moves through His church, searching people's hearts to see if they have those attitudes.

Lesson

L. Dependence

Put in negative terms, dependence is the attitude of insufficiency. It is sensing that you are not sufficient on your own. That kind of attitude is hard to develop in capable people. It's hard to develop in churches like Grace Church, because there are so many competent people getting things done. Our past accomplishments show that we can get things done, and that's what makes us lose our sense of dependence on God. If a church isn't careful, it can come to the point of eliminating God in its ministries because it's depending on the strength of its people and programs. That wouldn't happen so easily if we had the same problem as believers behind the Iron Curtain. They live daily in fear of death and have few resources. Those of us who have been abundantly blessed by God can easily forget Him. Remember when the Lord gave Israel the Promised Land? He gave them "great and goodly cities, which [they] buildest not, and houses full of all good things, which [they] filledst not, and wells digged, which [they] diggedst not" (Deut. 6:10*b*-11*a*). Yet they still forgot about God.

It's easy to get absorbed in activities, great ideas, and bright hopes. But we have to make sure that we don't get so involved in them that we do things that aren't in God's will. We must maintain an attitude of dependence on God.

1. Running ahead of God

    a) The danger of being presumptuous

    In Psalm 19, David said, "Keep back thy servant also from presumptuous sins" (v. 13*a*). It's so easy to do things without being dependent on God—without searching for the heart and mind of God. It is important that when you make decisions, you pray to the Lord with patience and commune with Him until you know that whatever you do will be the work of God. I've always had a fear of doing something in my ministry that the Lord wasn't a part of. I've always wanted to walk at the same pace that Christ does. I want to have the same goals that He has, because He is building the church, not I. I don't want to compete with Him. But it's so easy to be presumptuous and attempt to do things without God's help.

An Unforgettable Lesson on Being Presumptuous

When I went to Talbot Seminary, all the students had to preach at least twice in chapel. As we preached, members of the faculty sat behind us on a platform with critique sheets that they would fill out during the sermons. If a student was only ten minutes into his sermon, and he could hear the critique sheets being turned over in order to fill out the back, then he knew he was in trouble! Nevertheless, everyone tried his best.

I was assigned to preach on 2 Samuel 7. I wanted to make sure that I did a good job on it, so I literally memorized my sermon. I even memorized where my pauses were! I started my sermon by talking about David's desire to build a house for the ark of God. David felt bad because he lived in a beautiful palace while the ark of God was still in a tent. He told Nathan the prophet, "See, now, I dwell in an house of cedar, but the ark of God dwelleth within curtains" (v. 2). Nathan commended David and told him to go ahead and do what was on his heart (v. 3). But God in effect said, "David will not build a house for Me, for he is a man of war and has shed blood" (1 Chron. 28:3). Solomon was the one that would build the house of God (2 Sam. 7:12-13). Although God did not allow David to build His house, He did give him a wonderful promise (vv. 8-16).

Using those verses, I preached on the sin of presuming on God. It was a life-changing experience for me because that message has stuck in my mind through the years. When I finished preaching, one of the professors handed me his critique sheet. I opened it, and he hadn't even used it. Instead, he had written on it, "You missed the entire point of the passage." That ruined my day, but it was a very good lesson. The professor thought that I should have preached on the kingdom promise that God gave to David. I knew the passage talked about the kingdom promise, but I felt my own heart needed to hear about presumption, because I tend to move ahead too fast sometimes. Frequently I need to remind myself to be dependent on God—to seek His heart and mind. It just takes a few instances of going out on a limb without God and getting sawed off to help cure the problem of being presumptuous.

    b) The demand for being prayerful

        Prayer is a key element in preventing presumptuousness. A church must have a spirit of dependence.

When a church has many wonderful programs and ministries, it is easy to stop depending on God. There must be a sustained dependence, because God can easily choose to stop blessing us.

2. Running with God

    a) An example of dependency

        (1) The panic

            In John 14, we see a different aspect of dependence on God. Jesus was in the upper room, having His last discourse with His disciples before He left them. In that discourse, He gave them many wonderful promises because they were afraid of what would happen after he left. They had depended on Him for everything for three years. He made the food that fed them; He helped them pay their taxes; and He had told them everything they needed to know about the kingdom, God, man, sin, and righteousness. The disciples were troubled about Jesus' departure because they knew how dependent they were on Him.

        (2) The promise

            (a) Expressed

                While the disciples were becoming panicky, Jesus made them a wonderful promise: "Whatever ye shall ask in my name, that will I do, that the Father may be glorified in the Son. If ye shall ask anything in my name, I will do it" (vv. 13-14). Does that mean that Jesus will give us anything we ask for? No, He only gives what is asked for in His name. Some people think that if you say, "In Jesus' name," at the end of a prayer then you will get your request. But that's not what Jesus was talking about.

            (b) Explained

                In the Old Testament, God said that His name was "I AM THAT I AM" (Ex. 3:14). In other words, "My name is everything that I am." Christ's name is all that He is. So when you ask for something in His name, what you ask

83

for should be consistent with His will. If it is, then He will do what you ask. We need to learn to live in constant dependency on God and pray, "Lord, whatever You want, do it." If we do that, then we won't be bitter if something doesn't happen the way we want it to. That's how the Father is glorified, because then He is doing what He wants to do for His own glory. When we let God energize our ministry, then we know it's His ministry that is being carried on in the name of His Son.

b) An encouragement for dependency

(1) Praying for God's desire

I want the ministry at Grace Church to be God's ministry, not the ministry of clever, creative men. We should want the ministry of the Spirit of God in the name of the Son of God to be for the glory of God Himself. We need in our hearts a sense of insufficiency so that we are forced to depend on God and pray for whatever Jesus wants done. In Luke 11:2, when the disciples asked Jesus to teach them how to pray, He said, "When ye pray, say, Our Father, who art in Heaven, Hallowed be thy name." When you say, "Hallowed be thy name," then you are saying, "Lord, let your name be glorified and exalted." The prayer continues, "Thy kingdom come. Thy will be done, as in heaven, so in earth" (Luke 11:2b). We should pray that God will do on earth what He is doing in His heavenly kingdom. The Disciples' Prayer doesn't begin by saying, "Give us this and that." It starts out, "Hallowed be thy name. Thy kingdom come. Thy will be done." We should have that perspective; we have no right to ask for anything. That prayer teaches us to pray in a dependent way—to pray for God to do His work in His way.

(2) Praying for God's direction

It has always been the goal of Grace Church to let Christ build the church and be content just to be a part of it. But sometimes I'm afraid we may become so program oriented that we will forget to pray for God's will to be done until a disaster hits. As long as we ask God to guide us, then we won't have any problems. We don't want to do anything that God doesn't want us to do. That's why there needs to be an attitude of dependence. We have depended on God and His Word, and we have sought Him in prayer, but we can still improve our attitude of dependence. I think sometimes we get caught up in the milieu of contemporary Christianity and work more than we should and pray less than we should.

There's nothing more wonderful then spending time in prayer before doing something, and then doing it with a sense of freedom that lets you know you are walking side by side with the Savior as His will is being done. When I started teaching this series on the anatomy of a church, that's the feeling I had. I didn't know where the Lord was going to lead us as we studied together, but I sensed the companionship of Christ because I prayed to Him regarding what needed to be taught at this time about His church.

M. Flexibility

1. The hindrance caused by routine

We need to have the ability to change. Somebody once said that the seven last words of the church are, "We've never done it that way before!" That's really true.

a) The observance of tradition

In Matthew 15, some Pharisees and scribes came up to Jesus and confronted Him, saying, "Why do thy disciples transgress the tradition of the elders? For they wash not their hands when they eat bread" (v. 2). By that they meant that the disciples were not doing the required ceremonial rituals before they ate, not that they weren't washing their hands. Jesus responded, "Why do ye also transgress the commandment of God by your tradition?" (v. 3). We've all been obsessed with tradition at times. Some churches have so many traditions that they end up not being able to do what the Word of God commands. Sometimes a church will see a command in the Bible and say, "We can't do that; we must

85

maintain our tradition." Some churches have a style of ministry that is so unbiblical that when they are introduced to a command from God that goes against their traditions, they ignore it. There must be an attitude of flexibility in a church.

b) The objection to tradition

People often ask me to send them an organizational chart of Grace Church. That would be impossible, because things are always changing. God is always working through different people who at different times are strong, weak, very committed, or less committed. There are always new people joining the church, and God works through them. I think that the constant change is wonderful, because then we can't try to administrate things in our own power. People are always learning new things and becoming stronger in their Christian walk. That helps us avoid falling into routines that keep us from the reality of God's Word. We don't want tradition to get in the way if we learn something new about what God wants us to do.

c) The obsession with tradition

My wife had a distant relative that we used to visit during the holidays. The last time we visited her was during Christmastime. While we were visiting, she said, "John, do you have a Christmas Eve service at your church?" I said, "No we don't. We just encourage everybody to be at home with their families and talk about the meaning of Christmas and the birth of the Lord." She said, "That's too bad. At our church, we've *always* had a Christmas Eve service." I said, "Do you go to them?" She said, "No one goes, but we've *always* had a Christmas Eve service."

We humans are creatures of habit. If we have good habits, then that's great, but bad habits are hard to break. When people get used to a certain way of doing things, it is amazing how resistant they will be to change. But change is sometimes needed so people don't get confused between routine and reality. We need to be flexible because we depend on God. Sometimes He will do one thing in different ways. It grieves me to see a young pastor start teaching a church the Word of God and see the people of the church not respond because they are set in their routines. Such people will say, "We can't apply the Word of God in that situation because we'll upset a few people if we don't keep our tradition." They let the traditions of men stand in the way of the commandments of God.

2. The harmony that comes by resilience

a) In a church

I'm very grateful that at Grace Church we've been able to be flexible. When I began pastoring, and the congregation and I studied the Word of God together, we realized that certain things needed to be changed so that we would be in line with God's will. That attitude continues to prevail. Sometimes we send young pastors to other churches, and they come back saying, "I've tried to break down the wall of tradition at that church, but I don't know if the people there will ever change." We have to be flexible.

b) In a Christian

We need to be flexible in our personal lives, too. When Paul had finished his ministry in Galatia and Phrygia (cities that were in the area now known as Turkey), he wanted to go south into Asia (the seven churches of Asia Minor were there). He started in that direction, but the Holy Spirit stopped him (Acts 16:6). Paul didn't let that keep him from ministering somewhere else. He said to his companions, "We've already been east, and we can't go south, so let's go north to Bithynia." The Holy Spirit didn't allow that either (v. 7). The only direction they could go now was west, and the ocean was in that direction. Not knowing what to do, Paul probably prayed about where he should go. When he and his companions were asleep, Paul had a vision. In it was a man from Macedonia who said, "Come over into Macedonia, and that began the gospel's spread beyond the Middle East to the rest of the world. Paul was flexible about where God took him.

Some time ago, one of our elders, a Jewish Christian, became burdened to reach Jewish people for Christ. His desire was to go to Paris and reach out to the Jewish people there. He got involved in the Bible

Christian Union, a mission group that serves in France. They helped train and prepare him. A plaque was put up in my dad's church reminding everyone of his goal. But when he was ready to be used by God, the Lord placed him in Montreal, Canada. There are many French-speaking Jewish people there, just as there are in Paris. God had a different place in mind, and the missionary was flexible.

The church has to be flexible too. It has to be able to say, "God, we depend on You to lead us, and we're willing to move wherever You take us." Flexibility is an important attitude.

N. Growth

1. The passion for growth

It is important for us to have within us the desire to grow. First Peter 2:2 says, "As newborn babes, desire the pure milk of the word, that ye may grow by it." That analogy isn't talking about the milk of the Word as opposed to the meat (1 Cor. 3:2). Peter is simply saying, "In the same way babies desire milk, you must desire the Word so that you can grow." How much does a baby desire milk? If you've had a baby, you know that babies kick and scream when they want milk. They have a single-minded devotion to it. Peter says we're to have that same consuming desire for God's Word.

Do you ever hunger for the Word? Do you have to exert effort to open the Bible and read it, or is your heart magnetically drawn to it? Are you growing? We grow by feeding on the Word of God. We don't all have the same capacities to grow, but whatever capacity we do have, we should use to the fullest. Even though we have different abilities, the Spirit of God works in all of us to help us love His Word and grow at the proper pace. It would be terrible to hear people say, "I've had enough theology; I've heard so much exposition of the Scripture that I know more than I want to. I think I'll just leave." I pray that the people of Grace Church will never lose their desire to grow.

2. The process of growth

In 2 Peter 3:18, Peter says, "Grow in grace, and in the knowledge of our Lord and Savior, Jesus Christ." When we grow, we're not just learning facts in a book; we're

88

growing in the knowledge of our Lord and Savior Jesus Christ. We're getting to know Him. When you become born into the family of God, 1 John 2:13-14 says, you are a child and you know the Father (v. 13c). As you grow and become a spiritual young man, the Word of God dwells in you, and you "overcome the wicked one" (vv. 13b, 14b). First you know God in a simple way, then you become familiar with doctrine. When you are a spiritual father, then "ye have known him that is from the beginning" (vv. 13a, 14a). In other words, you're not just learning doctrine; you're learning to know God. The more you know God, the more enriching your fellowship with Him will be. Think of the most wonderful person you've ever met, and how it would be to have a friendship with him that continually grew. You should desire to have that kind of growing relationship with the infinite, holy God of the universe.

Do you have a hunger for the Word? Do you meditate on it? Do you feed on it daily? Can you say with Job that you love the Word of God more than your necessary food (Job 23:12b)? You should be growing. If you think you know a lot, you still don't know enough. You may know many facts from the Word of God, but do you know God as well as you should know Him? When I study a Bible passage, I always try to learn more about God's character so that I can get to know Him better.

O. Faithfulness

1. An enduring quality

Many Christians are spiritual sprinters—they get involved, serve for a while with all their energy, but then go into spriitual retirement. God is looking for marathon runners—people who will run a long distance. First Corinthians 4:2 says, "Moreover, it is required in stewards, that a man be found faithful." Long-term spiritual commitment is wonderful. A person in his eighties in our fellowship recently said to me, "Could you slow down when you preach? I'm having trouble keeping up taking notes." I love that! He's over eighty years old and still taking sermon notes! He's still excited about the Word, the life of God, and the church. He's faithful to the ministry. He hasn't quit in his commitment to God. It's the people who teach, disciple, and serve others for years that are the stalwarts of the faith. Their ministry is not based on an emotional appeal or a temporary response to a need; it's based upon their character. They have an enduring quality. Many people come to church only when it's convenient. Some people even serve for a while when it's convenient. But to them, service is low on their list of priorities. But those who are committed remain steadfast. We need to have that spirit of faithfulness. We need to have an enduring commitment.

In 2 Timothy 4:6-7, Paul says, "For I am now ready to be offered, and the time of my departure is at hand. I have fought a good fight, I have finished my course, I have kept the faith." What a great statement! He was saying, "I can die now; I'm done. I've finished the task God gave me. I've fought the fight and kept the faith." Those are wonderful words.

2. An elusive quality

It's sad when you see older Christians become indifferent about their commitment to God. Sometimes that happens to preachers, teachers, or other Christian workers when they become older. They become bitter and self-centered. It's beautiful to see a person grow old and continue in a life of faithful service. We all have the resonsibility to have faithful spirits and meet with the Lord's people regularly.

Not everybody that comes to Grace Church comes faithfully. If they did, that would be amazing. Sometimes when my wife and I go to a store, someone will come up to me and say, "I know you. You're John Mac-Arthur. I go to your church." I'll say, "How wonderful! I haven't seen you before. Were you there last Sunday?" The other person will say, "No, I wasn't there last Sunday. It's been a while since I've gone. But I love Grace Church." It makes me sad when people come to church only when it's convenient. A faithful Christian makes a priority of worshiping, serving, and praying consistently. It's sad when people are distracted by other things and don't keep their priorities right.

P. Hope

1. Rejoicing with an eternal perspective

Hope is a great word. For the Christian, *hope* means security for the future. There is no fear of death. We can actually look forward to what's ahead of us in life and death.

I love Paul's expression in Romans 12:12, "Rejoicing in hope." Death holds no fear for us. A funeral service for a Christian should be a cause for rejoicing and praising God because that person has gone from this place of tears, disease, death, and limitations to a place that's free of those things. We are saved by hope (Rom. 8:24a) and look forward to eternity, when we'll be like Christ. We look forward to the fulfillment of Romans 8:23, which says that we'll have redeemed bodies to go with our redeemed souls. We live in hope.

2. Refraining from an earthly perspective

It's important for us to have an attitude of hope. Practically speaking, that means we shouldn't become too obsessed with earthly things. Jesus said, "Lay not up for yourselves treasures upn earth, where moth and rust doth corrupt, and where thieves break through and steal . . . for where your treasure is, there will your heart be also" (Matt. 6:19-21). If our hearts are focusing on our hope in eternity, then our treasure is going to be in eternity, too. I hope you aren't living for the moment. Don't live for what is temporal. We should be living in hope, and that means we should be more committed to investing in eternity than investing in what is temporary. Our energy, thoughts, dreams, prayers, and money are only ours as a means to invest in an eternal reality. We live in hope; we live in the light of eternity. We have a wonderful future before us!

If all the attitudes that we've talked about are present in your church, then it *will* be all that Christ wants it to be.

Focusing on the Facts

1. What is Christ doing as He moves in His church? Why is it important to know that (see pp. 79-80)?
2. Put in negative terms, dependence is the attitude of _____ (see p. 81).
3. Why is an attitude of dependence hard for competent people to develop (see p. 81)?
4. What must you do before you make decisions so that you will know that what you are doing is the work of God (see p. 81)?
5. Why were Jesus' disciples afraid when He said He would leave them? What did He do to reassure them that everything would be all right (see p. 83)?

6. Explain what Jesus meant when he said, "If ye shall ask anything in my name, I will do it" (John 14:14; see pp. 83-84).
7. What perspective does the Disciples' Prayer teach us to have? How does it do that (Luke 11:2; see pp. 84-85)?
8. What can happen to a church that places great emphasis on tradition (see p. 86)?
9. Why would it be bad to try to keep the organizational structure of a church the same over an extended period of time (see p. 86)?
10. Why is change sometimes needed in a church (see p. 87)?
11. Explain how Paul showed flexibility in his circumstances (Acts 16:6-10; see pp. 87-88).
12. According to 1 Peter 2:2, what are we to desire? Why (see p. 88)?
13. What should we do with the capacity we have to grow? What does the Spirit of God do in all of our hearts (see p. 88)?
14. What is the nature of our growth, according to 2 Peter 3:18? Describe the steps of growth mentioned in 1 John 2:13-14 (see p. 89).
15. Describe spiritual sprinters. What kind of runner is God looking for? What is required of a steward, according to 1 Corinthians 4:2 (see p. 89)?
16. What things are the ministry of a committed person *not* based upon? What *is* it based upon (see p. 90)?
17. What does the word *hope* mean to a Christian? What does a Christian have to look forward to (see p. 91)?
18. To keep our perspective of hope, what should we refrain from doing (Matt. 6:19; see p. 91)?
19. As Christians, we should be living in hope. Consequently, to what should we be committed (see p. 91)?

Pondering the Principles

1. It is important for you to be dependent on God in all that you do. Write a list of the things you are currently doing in your church. Look at your list, and ask yourself these questions: How much do I pray about each of the things I am doing? Have I sought God's divine guidance whenever I needed to make a decision? How much do I depend on God in each of the things I am doing? Examine your life and make sure that you are depending on God in every aspect of your church life. If you are not dependent on God, then it is very easy to do things that are not a part of His will.

2. Describe how the people in the following passages were flexible: Genesis 12:1-5; Exodus 12:31-35; Judges 7:1-8; Ezra 10:2-3, 9-12; Psalm 139:23-24; Matthew 4:18-22; and Acts 9:1-22. Notice that in

each of those examples, willingness to be flexible was a response of obedience to God. Do you have any traditions or sins in your life that you have not been flexible enough to remove so that you are following God's commands? Why? Make sure that your life is characterized by a willingness to do whatever the Lord wants you to do.

3. If you were to draw a chart of your growth pattern as a Christian, what would it look like? Has your rate of growth continued to accelerate as you have matured in Christ? What specific steps are you taking now to maintain your growth as a Christian? To make sure that you are continually growing in Christ, specify the ways you plan to maintain your growth, and keep track of your progress at regular intervals.

4. Write a list of the different ways you have served in your church on a regular basis. How many of those things are you still doing? Next to the things that you aren't doing anymore, write how long you served in that capacity. Do you have a pattern of being involved in things for only a short period of time? For each of the things you aren't doing anymore, ask yourself why you stopped doing it. Do you find that your involvement may have been based on superficial things such as an emotional appeal or a temporary interest? Ask God for His guidance in your current areas of service, and make sure that you have a true, enduring commitment to what you are doing for His church.

5. How often do you think about your future life in eternity? What things are you doing now that show you are investing in eternity? Does the way you spend your time, money, and energy show that you are laying up for yourself treasures on earth? As a Christian, you have the privilege of rejoicing in the hope that you have before you. Don't allow earthly things to distract you!

6
The Anatomy of a Church—
Part 6
(The Muscles)

Outline

Introduction
 A. The Responsibility
 B. The Remembrance
Review
 I. The Skeleton
 II. The Internal Systems

Lesson
 III. The Muscles
   A. Preaching and Teaching
     1. The particulars
       a) The content described
       b) The commission delivered
       c) The clout demanded
       d) The commitment discussed
     2. The priority
       a) Paul's command to preach diligently
       b) Paul's command to preach confrontively
         (1) Preaching calls others to accountability
         (2) Preaching calls you to accountability
   B. Evangelism and Missions
     1. Evangelism
       a) Through our lives
         (1) The salt of the earth
         (2) The light of the world
       b) Through our words
     2. Missions
   C. Worshiping
     1. The discussion of worship
     2. The devotion to worship
     3. The definition of worship

D. Praying
1. It is selfless
    a) Praying for others
    b) Praying for ourselves
2. It is private

Introduction

God has blessed and built Grace Church. The people desire for the church to be all that He wants it to be. We are as rich in spiritual things as any church could be. Although we enjoy those blessings, it's important for us to understand the reasons that God blesses us with the best that He has to give. That's why in this study, we're doing a little spiritual archaeology and examining the foundations of Grace Church. We want to share what we're committed to.

A. The Responsibility

I rejoice in the Lord because I see God's work being done through the people at this church. I'm not doing this study because I believe we lack in the things a church should be committed to; rather, I want to encourage us to be more committed to those things. Paul said the same thing to the Thessalonians about love: "As touching brotherly love, ye need not that I write unto you; for ye yourselves are taught of God to love one another. And, indeed, ye do it toward all the brethren who are in all Macedonia. But we beseech you, brethren, that ye increase more and more" (1 Thess. 4:9-10). However, my fear is that as the church grows, people will get further away from the foundational things that it is built upon. If that happens, then we will decline in our usefulness to God and His blessings on us will decrease. The virtues we have studied are present in the hearts of the people and the ministries at our church. But I still want to call everyone to a greater commitment to those virtues.

All of us have a great responsibility to make sure others see those virtues in us. I believe there are principles that place a church in a position of maximum blessing by God. It's not the largeness of a church that counts; it's the attitude of the people that is important. It's the commitment in our lives that other people must see. It's the things in us as committed believers that aren't always seen in others who call themselves Christians that make us useful to God. The purpose of this study, *The Anatomy of a Church*, is to see what things make a church all that it should be. We have to keep reminding ourselves what makes up the foundation of a church.

B. The Remembrance

Peter said, "Wherefore, I will not be negligent to put you always in remembrance of these things, though ye know them, and are established in the present truth" (2 Pet. 1:12). Although the people he was writing to already knew what they should know, he wanted to make sure they remembered. You have to keep on track. It's easy to start down a track and all of a sudden go off on a different path. You have to remember God's truth so that you don't wander from it.

Review

In our study about the church, we've been making features of the human body to be analogous to the church.

I. THE SKELETON (see pp. 9-17)

II. THE INTERNAL SYSTEMS (see pp. 24-91)

A body must have internal systems that give it life. They give the body the capability to act and react. The church's internal systems are made up of certain spiritual attitudes. It's what's flowing in the lives of the people in a church that is important. We tell pastors that look at Grace Church, "Don't just take what you see on the surface here and try to incorporate it in your church at home. Behind the surface of things are certain internal attitudes that have to be built into people's hearts before a ministry can be what God wants it to be."

Lesson

III. THE MUSCLES

The muscles represent the function of a body. The body gets its form from its skeleton and its life from its internal systems. The muscles enable it to function. What are the functions of the church? What are its responsibilities? What should our ministries be? After a church has become committed to worshiping God, the authority of Scripture, teaching sound doctrine, personal holiness, submitting to spiritual authority, and cultivating proper spiritual attitudes, what is it supposed to do?

We are going to look now at the responsibilities of the church. I call these the muscles—the things that make the church move.

A. Preaching and Teaching

I've put preaching and teaching together because they both are related to the proclamation of biblical truth. I see the proclamation of the Word as a primary function of the church. The church is the receiver of the revelation of God; therefore, it must be the dispenser of it as well. God has revealed Himself to us so that we will understand Him. We, then, are to be hearers and proclaimers of His Word.

I am committed to that as an absolute priority in the church. Proclaiming the Word of God is a function of the church. I grieve over the sermonettes that people hear in some churches. Some preachers just counsel and deal with ethical issues from the pulpit. There are many Sunday school classes at different churches where people don't really know much about the Bible, and they guess about what it teaches. But the church's most important function is to proclaim the Word of God in an understandable, direct, authoritative way.

1. The particulars

Let's look now at excerpts from the two epistles that Paul wrote to Timothy. Those epistles were written to help us understand the ministry from the viewpoints of the minister and the congregation. In fact, 1 Timothy 3:15 says that 1 Timothy was written to tell us "how thou oughtest to behave thyself in the house of God [the church]." Both 1 and 2 Timothy emphasize that we are to make a priority of proclaiming the Word of God.

a) The content described

First Timothy 3:16 talks about the wonder of the incarnation of Jesus Christ: "Without controversy great is the mystery of godliness: God was manifest in the flesh." That's an amazing truth. It's the heart of the Christian faith. If God hadn't manifested himself in the flesh of Jesus Christ to die and rise again, then our faith would mean nothing. The incarnation is the very heart of our faith—it is a great revealed truth.

Reading further, Paul said: "God was manifest in the flesh, jusitifed in the Spirit, seen of angels, preached unto the nations, believed on in the world, received up into glory." Notice the words "preached unto the nations" (v. 16). One of the essential elements of

God's manifesting Himself in the flesh is preaching. There must be a proclamation of the incarnation. I believe that at the heart of the church is the incarnation, and at the heart of the incarnation is its proclamation. Preaching has a central place in the life of a church.

b) The commission delivered

Paul told Timothy to be faithful to preach. He said, "If thou put the brethren in remembrance of these things" (1 Tim. 4:6). In other words, "Timothy, your primary responsibility is to be a teacher. Whatever you've received from God's Spirit, teach that to the church. Teach the brethren the truth of God." How marvelous it is that we can tell people that the Bible is God's truth! So many are groping for truth, making up their own opinions about things and trying to figure out the meaning to life. Pilate, the ultimate cynic of the New Testament, said, "What is truth?" (John 18:38a). We know the truth. Jesus said to the Father in John 17, "Thy word is truth" (v. 17b). What a legacy! We must impart God's truth.

I believe that God has blessed Grace Church because we have made a priority of proclaiming the Word of God. We don't just talk about the Bible; we teach from it. Many hundreds of people over the years have said they come to Grace Church because they want to be fed the Word of God. That's our commitment; that's our function. It isn't just my job to proclaim the Word; it's everybody's job! Some people are gifted to preach or teach, but we're all to proclaim the Word.

c) The clout demanded

Paul told Timothy that if he reminded the brethren of the truth, that he would be "a good minister of Jesus Christ, nourished up in the words of faith and of good doctrine" (1 Tim. 4:6). Paul adds in verse 11, "These things command and teach." In other words, "Teach with authority."

I was invited to speak at a commencement ceremony at the Los Angeles Police Academy recently, and the man next to me told me about the various graduates. He said, "We had to flunk one man because of his voice. It wasn't authoritative enough. A policeman needs to have authority in his voice." I thought that was interesting. A policeman's authority is the law. If I sound like I speak with authority, it's because the authority is the Word of God. That's what Paul was emphasizing to Timothy in 1 Timothy 4:11: "You don't just teach the Word; you command it. You call people to a mandate of responsibility." In verse 13 Paul continues "Till I come, give attendance to reading, to exhortation, to doctrine." Timothy was to read the Bible, explain its doctrines, and exhort people to apply them. He was told not to neglect preaching (v. 14), but to meditate upon God's truths (v. 15), take heed to them, and continue in them (v. 16). The responsibility we all have to proclaim the Bible is thrilling.

Preaching: The Focal Point of the Church

Paul talks about another dimension of preaching and teaching in 1 Timothy 5:17. He said, "Let the elders that rule well be counted worthy of double honor, especially they who labor in the word and doctrine." That verse tells us that the leadership of a church should focus on preaching and teaching. The church's function is to proclaim God's Word.

I've heard people criticize Grace Church by saying, "There's too much preaching and teaching at Grace Church and not enough of other things." I don't see how there could ever be too much preaching and teaching. That could happen if everyone knew all of God's revelation, but that is impossible. There can't be too much proclamation of the Word. The only way we would have too much preaching and teaching is if people didn't obey what they were taught. The reason we put so much emphasis on preaching and teaching is because they help everything else to happen. We have to know what the Bible says about something before we know how to act. Teaching is the *sine qua non* of everything. We won't know how to worship, pray, evangelize, discipline, shepherd, train, or serve unless we know what the Word of God says. That's why preaching and teaching are so important.

d) The commitment discussed

In 1 Timothy 6, Paul tells Timothy "Keep that which is committed to thy trust" (v. 20). In other words, he was telling Timothy to hold onto the revelation of

God—the content of true doctrine—and stay away from the philosophies and errant theologies of the world. Likewise, we are to be careful not to deviate from God's Word. We don't want to get carried away by the opinions of men.

In 2 Timothy 2:15, Paul tells Timothy, "Study to show thyself approved unto God, a workman that needeth not to be ashamed, rightly dividing the word of truth." Paul wanted Timothy to handle the Word correctly. In 2 Timothy 1:13, he says, "Hold fast the form of sound words." A person proclaiming God's Word must commit himself to it and then dispense it. Paul told Timothy to be committed to the Word, preach it, and stay away from the heresies of the world (2 Tim. 2:16). Paul adds in 2:24 that a servant of the Lord—a leader in the church—must be "apt to teach." He must be skilled in his teaching. According to 2 Timothy 3:16-17, it is Scripture that perfects us; that includes enabling a person to preach and teach.

As you can see, Paul emphasized to Timothy the importance of preaching and teaching in the church.

2. The priority

a) Paul's command to preach diligently

Paul gives a great mandate to Timothy in 2 Timothy 4:1-2. He says, "I charge thee, therefore" (v. 1a). The word *therefore* points back to what Paul has just said in 3:16-17: "Since the Word of God is able to make people understand salvation, and is able to make you perfect in Christ, 'I charge thee . . . before God, and the Lord Jesus Christ, who shall jusge the living and the dead at his appearing and his kingdom: Preach the word" (2 Tim. 4:1-2a). Paul held Timothy accountable before God to preach the Word. It is Scripture that makes people "wise unto salvation" (2 Tim. 3:15b). It is the Word that "is profitable for doctrine, for reproof, for correction, for instruction in righteousness, that the man of God may be perfect, thoroughly furnished unto all good works" (vv. 16-17). Continuing in 2 Timothy 4:2, Paul said, "Preach the word; be diligent in season, out of season." In other words, "Work hard at proclaiming God's Word. Keep preaching all the time. Don't worry about whether people are offended by what you say."

b) Paul's command to preach confrontively

(1) Preaching calls others to accountability

Paul tells Timothy in 2 Timothy 4:2, "Reprove, rebuke, exhort." Why did Paul say that? Because he knew that Christians are always fighting their sin. He knew that preaching needed to be confrontive. The mildest of the three confrontive words is "exhort," which means "to encourage a person to change his behavior and warn of judgment if he doesn't change." Preaching has to confront people about their sin. It must cause people to search their hearts and feel convicted.

Paul told Timothy to be confrontive in his preaching and to do it "with all long-suffering and doctrine" (v. 2b). Preaching should be done with conviction. It should make people look at the failures in their lives. However, we can't expect people to change overnight. In the process of confrontive preaching, we must be patient and teach doctrine. It is the Word that convicts. One of the functions of the church is to patiently teach the Word of God in a confrontive way so that people are made accountable before God to make sure their lives are right.

(2) Preaching calls you to accountability

You yourself are called to that accountability. When you go to church or Bible study and listen to the teaching, you are being called by the authority of the Word of God to see if you are living according to the Scriptures. If your life is not right, then the preaching will reprove or rebuke you until your life is what God wants it to be.

So, when Paul gave what were his last instructions to Timothy, he said, "Everything is summed up in this command: Preach the word." You say, "Why is that?" Because it's when people have the Word in their minds that right behavior is generated. Ephesians 4:23 says, "Be renewed in the spirit of your mind." Romans 12:2 says, "Be not conformed to this world, but be ye transformed by the renewing of your mind." You need to have the Word in your mind so that you are able to produce right behavior. Preaching and teaching the Word helps put Scripture in people's minds; there is no substitute for them.

B. Evangelism and Missions

I use the terms *evangelism* and *missions* together just to give you a comprehensive perspective. Evangelism is generally carried out on a personal basis, while mission work usually covers broad areas. We are to be committed to the fact that the church exists for the sake of the world. We are to desire to live as God wants us to so we can be shining lights in the midst of a dark and perverse generation (Phil. 2:15). The ultimate goal of all ministry is to reach others for Christ.

1. Evangelism

There are two ways to evangelize: through our lives and through our words.

a) Through our lives

It's our lives that make our testimonies believable or unbelievable. If we have a church where Christ is exalted and people are living in obedience to God, then we're going to establish credibility for our testimonies. The way we live in the world is important.

It's wonderful when people come to Grace Church and say, "The people here really live out their message. They obey the Word of God." Living out the Bible is what makes Christianity credible. Have you ever noticed that Satan doesn't try to destroy the church through extermination but through proliferating churches that have no credibility? He knows that doing that will undermine the message of the gospel. How many times have you heard people say things like, "I went to that church over there, and they have a lot of hypocrites. They don't care about anyone. The pastor embezzled money from the church and ran off"? Satan does everything he can to corrupt churches so that the integrity of the gospel message is undermined. He wants to corrupt churches so that there is no foundation for individual testimonies.

I believe that we have been called to live an evangelistic life-style in our communities. In Matthew 5:13, our Lord says that we are:

(1) The salt of the earth

Jesus said, "But if the salt have lost its savor, with what shall it [the earth] be salted?" (Matt. 5:13). We are a preservative on the earth; we are distinct. That's why we're called to live pure lives. I am concerned that we live godly, virtuous lives not just so that we can glorify God, but so that unbelievers can glorify God. We are to live holy lives because that will draw others to that kind of purity. We are to be godly examples.

(2) The light of the world

Matthew 5:15 says that a light is not supposed to be hidden under a bushel. The word *bushel* is used to indicate that there is sin in your life or that you are clouding the testimony of your life; consequently, your light is not shining.

If you're really salting the earth and shining brightly, then you're going to have an impact on the world. Your actions speak louder than words: "Let your light so shine before men, that they may see your good works, and glorify your Father, who is in heaven" (Matt. 5:16).

Are You Hurting the Credibility of Christianity?

I have met people I know in circumstances that were embarrassing to them. I can't tell you how many people have tried to swallow a cigarette when they saw me! Sometimes I'll go into a restaurant and see someone I know with a drink in his hand. I'll just smile and wave, and he'll go into instant panic. I don't have to say anything. On some occasions, I've even gone over to a table and greeted people I know just to remind them that there is a certain standard of life for Christians to live up to for the sake of unbelievers that watch us.

One time when I went into a restaurant, a cocktail waitress came up to me and said, "Would you like a cocktail?" I knew her, and when she recognized me, she was embarrassed and said, "No, you wouldn't want a cocktail." I said, "You look familiar." She said, "I have to apologize," and gave me a story about why she was a cocktail waitress. But it was very interesting because she knew that she was not living the

Christian testimony she was supposed to. It was embarrassing for her to see me. I thought, *She should be more embarrassed by unbelievers seeing her unChristian behavior than by my seeing it.* We have a foundation of credibility that we need to protect.

Jesus summed up your responsibility to live a righteous life when He said, "Let your light so shine before men, that they may see your good works, and glorify your Father, who is in heaven" (Matt. 5:16). Unbelievers should be able to look at your life and say, "Only God could do that in a person's life. What a wonderful life!"

b) Through our words

Not only do we need to live out the gospel, but we also need to proclaim it. We need to "be ready always to give an answer to every man that asketh [us] a reason of the hope that is in [us]" (1 Pet. 3:15). In order to proclaim Jesus Christ, we need to have our lips unsealed. Someone once joked that most Christians are like an Arctic river: they are frozen over at the mouth. It's unfortunate that for many Christians that is true. For some reason, many Christians are resistant to proclaiming Christ. We ought to be as eager to speak about the Lord as we are to speak about mundane things. One reason some of us have difficulty proclaiming the gospel is that we don't know very many non-Christians. Our world is narrowed. It's like a pyramid: the longer you've been a Christian, the fewer non-Christians you know.

When we proclaim the gospel, we have to make sure we know what to say. That's why at Grace Church we spend a lot of time articulating the gospel. We want to make sure everyone understands how a person becomes saved. We study how Christ evangelized the rich young ruler in Matthew 19:16-26 and the crowd that listened to His Sermon on the Mount (Matt. 5-7). Churches all over the world are filled with people who think they are saved, but they aren't because they misunderstand how a person obtains salvation. That's why we need to be committed to evangelism.

2. Missions

Missions is a worldwide view of outreach—it involves reaching across the globe to whatever areas God will open to us. I received a letter from a pastor in the Philippines, and he said, "I've heard about Grace Church. I want to build my church the way God would want it built. Could you send me some information so that I know what to do?" We have some people at our church strategizing for us to reach as far beyond our own walls as God will allow us. Jesus said, "Go ye, therefore, and teach all nations, baptizing them in the name of the Father, and of the Son, and of the Holy Spirit, teaching them to observe all things whatsoever I have commanded" (Matt. 28:19-20a). We want to reach out to the world as far as our resources permit. We are training people so that we can reach out more effectively. We're committed to preaching, baptizing, and teaching wherever we can.

C. Worshiping

1. The discussion of worship

Paul told the Philippians, "For we are the circumcision, who worship God in the spirit, and rejoice in Christ Jesus, and have no confidence in the flesh" (Phil. 3:3). John 4:23 says that those who "worship the Father in spirit and in truth" are true worshipers. We are called to offer our bodies as a living sacrifice to God in a holy act of worship (Rom. 12:1b). Peter said that we are "an holy priesthood, to offer up spritual sacrifices, acceptable to God by Jesus Christ" (1 Pet. 2:5).

2. The devotion to worship

At one of our church staff meetings recently, there was some concern about how many people really worship God during the service. These questions came up: How many hearts are really lifted up to God in praise and adoration? How many people are thinking about their plans for the rest of the day while the service is taking place? We are so bombarded by the cleverness of Satan's media—we continually think about shows we've watched or commercial tunes we've heard—that it's hard for us to push the clutter out of our minds so that we can meditate on the things of God.

3. The definition of worship

When you go to church, do you really think about the songs you are singing or meditate on the things of God that you hear taught and preached? Cultivate a worshipful heart. Your worship of God should not be confined to when you're in church. A worship service should just be a catalyst to get you to worship at all times. And we worship best when we are fully obedient. Obedience is the basic definition of worship. We are to obediently offer God praise, do what He says, and worship Him. Like obedience, worship should become a way of life rather than just an exercise on Sunday.

Hebrews 10:22 tells us to draw near to God. Do you know what it means to draw near to God? James 4:8 says, "Draw near to God, and he will draw near to you." What great thoughts those are! Do you ever draw near to God in an unhurried way? Do you let your heart and mind ascend when you hear the hymns, Scripture readings, or prayer? Do you meditate in deep devotion? Some people get a mental picture of gurus when they hear the word *meditate*. They don't know what it really means to meditate on God.

We function in worship. Paul told Timothy to have men lift up their hands in prayer (1 Tim. 2:8). The church is to meet together for the purpose of praise. We are to be worshipful people.

D. Praying

I believe with all my heart that prayer is the hardest spiritual exercise we engage in. There are two reasons for that.

1. It is selfless

   a) Praying for others

      Prayer is hard work because it is selfless. True prayer embraces the kingdom of God: "Our Father, who art in heaven, Hallowed be thy name. Thy kingdom come. Thy will be done" (Matt. 6:9b-10a). True prayer also embraces the people of God: "Give *us* this day *our* daily bread. And forgive *us our* debts, as *we* forgive *our* debtors. And lead *us* not into temptation" (Matt. 6:11-13a, italics added). There is no "I" in the Disciples' Prayer. That prayer embraces the kingdom of God, His glory, and the needs of His people. That's why prayer is an unselfish exercise. Only humble people can abandon themselves to embrace the will of God and the needs of His people. When Paul said in Ephesians 6:18 for us to be "praying always with all prayer and supplication in the Spirit," he was calling us to pray unselfishly for God's glorious will and the needs of His people. Prayer is selfless; only unselfish people can pray.

b) Praying for ourselves

It's hard work to pray on behalf of God, His will, and His people. It's easy for us to pray when a problem hits us. When we get injured, get sick, lose a loved one, get caught doing something wrong, despair over a child that strays from the Lord, or are concerned about whom our children are going to marry, then we find it easy to pray on our own behalf.

A person who prays only in times of personal need has a weak prayer life. A person has a strong prayer life when he is able to abandon himself in unceasing prayer on behalf of the glory of God in His eternal kingdom and the needs of His redeemed people. Luke 11:5-8 tells of a man banging on his friend's door for bread so that he could feed a guest. If I were hungry myself, I would have no problem banging on somebody's door all night for bread. But would I be able to bang on somebody's door all night for bread for somone else? A church can have an ice cream social after a service, and many people will show up. But if that same church has a prayer meeting, you would find that few would come. Not many people are selfless enough to pray. When we pray, we should embrace things other than ourselves. None of us pray as we should.

Why Do Older People Often Pray Better?

One of the benefits of growing older is that you have a longer list of answered prayers than younger people. You've had more chances to see God demonstrate His power. The more you see God answer prayer, the more confident you become in your prayers. I think that older people pray better than younger people because they have seen a larger number of God's responses to prayer.

2. It is private

This is another reason prayer is difficult. Usually you pray by yourself. No one knows how much you pray. That's why you've got to be self-disciplined to pray without peer pressure. Don't pray just so you can tell someone that you prayed. Some people go to a Bible study to look good or read a particular passage so they can say they've read that passage.

No one sees you when you pray. There are no visible rewards. We perform much better when we know people are watching us. I spend a great amount of time preparing my sermons because I know that many people are going to listen to what I say. But it's easy not to pray, because no one would notice the effects of that for a while. But if I come to church on Sunday without anything to say, then I'd be in trouble.

Prayer is hard work. It's selfless, and it's to be done without seeking people's attention or approval. I thank God for the selfless people we have in our church. We have a small group of older people that get together every Monday to pray. They've been praying together for more than ten years. They pray, and God answers their prayers. The church benefits from their faithfulness. Prayer is the nerve that moves the muscles of omnipotence. I don't know how to explain God's sovereignty and our prayer requests working together, but I do know that God answers prayer. James said, "The effectual, fervent prayer of a righteous man availeth much" (5:16b). I want to be a prayerful, righteous person because I want to see God do His work and give Him the glory due Him.

We must be committed to prayer. Paul couldn't have said that more clearly than when he said, "Pray without ceasing" (1 Thess. 5:17). What does it mean to pray unceasingly? Praying without ceasing means continually being conscious of God. It means offering your whole life as a prayer; that is, being aware of God every time you think, act, or talk. Every thought in life should be offered to God in prayer, as if to say, "I'm going to do this, Lord. Is that all right?" To pray unceasingly means to live life as if you were looking through the mind and heart of God. It doesn't mean walking around mumbling with your eyes closed all the time. Prayer allows us to communicate everything to God. Prayer works two ways: God speaks to us through prayer and leads us by His Spirit; we offer Him our thoughts, joys, and problems. Prayer is living life in a God-conscious way.

The functions of the church are foundational: preaching and teaching, evangelism and missions, worshiping, and praying.

Focusing on the Facts

1. What did Peter say in 2 Peter 1:12? Why (see p. 97)?
2. In our analogy of the body representing the church, what do the muscles represent (see p. 97)?
3. Why do preaching and teaching appear together as a function of the church (see p. 98)?
4. The church is the _____ of the revelation of God: therefore, it must be the _____ of it as well (see p. 98).
5. How is the church to proclaim the Word of God (see p. 98)?
6. Why was 1 Timothy written (1 Tim. 3:15)? What do 1 and 2 Timothy tell us (see p. 98)?
7. According to 1 Timothy 3:16, what must we proclaim (see pp. 98-99)?
8. What was Timothy's primary responsibility (1 Tim. 4:6; see p. 99)?
9. What was Paul emphasizing to Timothy in 1 Timothy 4:11 (see p. 99)?
10. What did Paul mean when he told Timothy, "Keep that which is committed to thy trust" (1 Tim. 6:20; see pp. 100-101)?
11. What charge did Paul make to Timothy in 2 Timothy 4:1-2? To whom did Paul hold Timothy accountable (see p. 101)?
12. Why did Paul tell Timothy to "Reprove, rebuke, exhort" (2 Tim. 4:2)? What does the word *exhort* mean there (see p. 102)?
13. About what must preaching confront people? How are we to confront others (see p. 102)?
14. What happens when people have the Word in their minds (see p. 102)?
15. What is the difference between evangelism and missions? What ultimate goal do they have in common (see p. 103)?
16. How can we establish credibility for our testimonies (see p. 103)?
17. Explain how Satan tries to destroy the church (see p. 103).
18. What will happen if we are the salt of the earth and light of the world (see p. 104)?
19. According to 1 Peter 3:15, what must we be ready to do at all times (see p. 105)?
20. What is one reason that some of us have difficulty proclaiming the gospel (see p. 105)?
21. How far into the world are we to venture with the gospel? Support your answer with Scripture (see p. 106).
22. Should your worship be confined to when you're in church? Explain (see p. 107).
23. When do we worship best (see p. 107)?
24. What is the first reason that it's hard to pray? What does true prayer embrace? Support your answer with Scripture (see pp. 107-8).

25. What does a person with a strong prayer life pray for (see p. 108)?
26. Why do older people often pray better (see p. 108)?
27. Explain the second reason that it's hard to pray (see p. 109).
28. What does "pray without ceasing" mean (1 Thess 5:17; see p. 109)?

Pondering the Principles

1. One of the primary functions of the church is to preach and teach the Bible. If you are responsible for preaching and teaching, estimate how much you use the Scripture in your teaching. Is everything you teach backed up by the Word of God? When you teach, do you teach *from* the Word, or do you just talk about it? How often do you interject your own opinions in your teaching material? How well do you know the material that you teach? If you do not handle God's Word correctly and carefully when you teach, then you will cause people to misunderstand it. Make sure that you are a "workman that needeth not to be ashamed, rightly dividing the word of truth" (2 Tim. 2:15).

2. Are you living an evangelistic life-style? A good way to answer that question is to ask yourself this: Is there anything in my life that I don't want my pastor or Christian friends to know about? If unbelievers know that you are a Christian and see you sin, what effect will that have on them? What effect will that have on the unbelievers' view of other Christians and the church? Read Matthew 5:16, and examine your life to see if you are bringing glory to God by the way you live.

3. When you worship God, do you find yourself easily distracted by unimportant thoughts during church services or devotion times? What can you do to prevent that from happening? One good idea is to start praying and meditating on God before you go to church. Describe your worship of God. What can you do to cultivate a more worshipful heart?

4. In your own words, write what it means to "pray without ceasing" (1 Thess. 5:17). Why do you think it is important for you to pray unceasingly?

111

7
The Anatomy of a Church—
Part 7
(The Muscles and the Flesh)

Outline

Introduction
A. The Accountability Stated
B. The Accountability Specified
  1. The requirements
     a) Being a servant
     b) Being faithful
     c) Being objective
  2. The restatement

Review
 I. The Skeleton
 II. The Internal Systems
III. The Muscles
  A. Preaching and Teaching
  B. Evangelism and Missions
  C. Worshiping
  D. Praying

Lesson
  E. Discipling
  1. The definition
  2. The description
     a) Introduced
     b) Illustrated
        (1) Evangelism
        (2) Love
        (3) Admonishment
        (4) Guidance
        (5) Teaching
  3. The dedication
  4. The destination

F. Shepherding
    1. The applications of shepherding
    2. The availability in shepherding
    3. The activity of shepherding
    4. The accountability in shepherding
G. Building Up Families
    1. The persecution by Satan
    2. The preservation by the Spirit
H. Training
I. Giving
    1. The principle explained
    2. The practice examined
        a) Giving meagerly
        b) Giving properly
J. Fellowshiping

IV. The Flesh

Introduction

My life is the church. I don't have a nine-to-five job; my job never ends. A minister of the Lord Jesus Christ never stops working. As believers, none of us stop working. Every waking moment of my life has to do with God's kingdom, work, people, and Word. Those things totally saturate my life.

A. The Accountability Stated

I've been given a unique calling. I understand that and with gratitude express my appreciation to God. Although there's great joy and wonderful privilege involved in ministering, there's also a serious and weighty responsibility. I'm often reminded of different heart-searching passages in Scripture related to the responsibility I have. James 3:1 says, "My brethren, be not many teachers, knowing that we shall receive the greater judgment." James is saying, "Don't be in a hurry to be in a position of spiritual responsibility unless you are ready to deal with the consequence of failure." Hebrews 13:17 says that spiritual leaders "watch for your souls, as they that must give account." Spiritual leaders are accountable to the Lord for the people they lead. There is serious accountability in shepherding the church of Jesus Christ. Even though there is great joy and blessedness derived from shepherding, there is also a lingering sense of the immense seriousness involved in leading a church.

B. The Accountability Specified

First Corinthians 4 gives us a perspective of the accountability involved in ministry. In that chapter Paul shares with the Corinthians about his place in the ministry.

1. The requirements

a) Being a servant

Paul says in verse 1, "Let a man so account of us, as of the ministers [Gk., *hupēretēs,* 'underrower,' or the lowest of slaves] of Christ, and stewards of the mysteries of God." In other words, he was saying, "When the time comes to evaluate us, let it be said that we were servants of Christ and stewards of the mysteries of God." The "mysteries of God" are those great truths that God imparted to Paul in the New Testament, and a steward is someone who manages something owned by someone else. Paul wanted to be thought of as a slave of Christ and a steward who aptly managed the truths of God.

b) Being faithful

Verse 2 continues, "Moreover, it is required in stewards, that a man be found faithful." Paul wanted to be a faithful slave of Christ. He wanted to handle in a trustworthy way what the Lord gave him. He was faithful to God's call.

c) Being objective

Paul says in verse 3, "But with me it is a very small thing that I should be judged of you, or of man's judgment; yea, I judge not mine own self." Paul wasn't concerned about other people's opinions of him. He wasn't even concerned about his own opinion of himself. The reason he wasn't concerned was that no one really knew his heart. He knew that he didn't know his own heart either, because his sinfulness made him blind to some of his weaknesses. The Corinthians couldn't judge Paul, and he couldn't judge himself.

Paul adds in verse 4, "For I know nothing against myself, yet am I not hereby justified; but he that judgeth me is the Lord." Paul was aware that even if he couldn't find a flagrant sin in his life, that didn't justify him. He knew that only the Lord could judge him.

2. The restatement

    Summed up, Paul said, "I'm in the ministry, and let it be said that I was a slave of Christ and a steward of the mysteries of God. I'm not concerned about the judgment of men because men don't know my heart. I'm not concerned about trying to evaluate myself because I am biased and don't know all about myself. The One that judges me is the Lord." Everyone that serves Christ will be judged by the Lord. We must all appear before the judgment seat of Christ to receive judgment for the things we've done, whether they were good or useless.

    Paul says in verse 5, "Therefore, judge nothing before the time, until the Lord come, who both will bring to light the hidden things of darkness, and will make manifest the counsels of the hearts." The real issue in serving Christ is what's in your heart. God won't judge you based on your cleverness or how dynamic a leader you were. God will evaluate your heart. Other people can't see your heart, and even you aren't always able to know your own heart. When the Lord makes "manifest the counsels of the hearts . . . then shall every man have praise of God" (v. 5*b*).

So, I confess to you that ministering to the church carries with it a great amount of seriousness for me. I am under double condemnation for my failures, as well as all others who minister and teach the Word. I must give an account to God for how I have shepherded and fed the flock. Ultimately, I will be judged by the Lord Himself. I don't want to live under the illusion that I can be satisfied with kind evaluations from men or a positive self-evaluation. I'm sharing with you from my heart the burdens that I bear—that everyone who serves Christ bears. I need you to bear that load with me.

Review

We've been talking about what God wants to see in His church. It is important to understand that those things are not optional. We've been using Paul's analogy of a body and looking at the church in a topical way. The church, like a body, can be divided into four elements: the skeleton, the internal systems, the muscles, and the flesh.

I. THE SKELETON (see pp. 9-17)

116

II. THE INTERNAL SYSTEMS (see pp. 24-91)

III. THE MUSCLES

The muscles represent the functions of the church. Once we understand our foundation and have the right spiritual attitudes, then we need to know what to do. We need to know the functions of the church—how it ministers and operates. Let's review the functions we've already studied:

A. Preaching and Teaching (see pp. 98-103)

In 2 Timothy 4:2, Paul instructed Timothy, "Preach the word." In that same verse, Paul also said, "Reprove, rebuke, exhort with all long-suffering and doctrine." Preaching and teaching are basic functions of the church.

B. Evangelism and Missions (see pp. 103-6)

Christ mandated that we "go . . . into all the world, and preach the gospel to every creature" (Mark 16:15). Paul said, "Knowing, therefore, the terror of the Lord, we persuade men" (2 Cor. 5:11a). In other words, because we know the impending doom on the ungodly, we are to warn them. We're called to evangelism and missions.

C. Worshiping (see pp. 106-7)

We are to be worshipers, both individually and corporately. We are to worship in the heart: "We are the circumcision, who worship God in the spirit, and rejoice in Christ Jesus, and have no confidence in the flesh" (Phil. 3:3). We are to be true worshipers that "worship him in spirit and in truth" (John 4:24). We are the temple of the Spirit of God (1 Cor. 3:16); God dwells within the praises of His redeemed people (Ps. 22:3). We worship not only individually but collectively. Hebrews 10:22 tells us to draw near to God with a pure heart.

D. Praying (see pp. 107-10)

The church is to be functioning in prayer. That is a priority. When Paul described the armor of the believer in Ephesians 6:10-17, notice that he ends in verse 18 with the words "Praying always." Prayer is the ultimate weapon of the believer. Even with the armor that I have available to me, I am still utterly dependent on God in prayer. When I have all of my armor on and the sword of the Spirit in my hand, I still need to pray. No matter what I may know or who I am, I cannot function independently of God, who is my power source. I must be praying always.

117

In the early church, the apostles said, "We will give ourselves continually to prayer, and to the ministry of the word" (Acts 6:4). Prayer is mentioned first because it's a priority. We must always be linked with God. If not, then we are operating in the flesh, and the flesh can't do anything good. Paul emphasized to Timothy the priority of prayer when explaining how to set the church in order: "I exhort, therefore, that first of all, supplications, prayers, intercessions, and giving of thanks, be made for all men" (1 Tim. 2:1). He also said, "I will, therefore, that men pray everywhere, lifting up holy hands" (v. 8*a*).

Lesson

E. Discipling

1. The definition

   In Matthew 28:19-20, our Lord said, "Go therefore and make disciples [Gk. *mathēteusate*, 'make learners,' or 'make disciples'] of all the nations, baptizing them . . . teaching them to observe all that I commanded you" (NASB). Discipling, then, is bringing people to Christ. Jesus was involved in discipling. In Matthew 27:57, we read that Joseph of Armiathea was discipled by Him.

2. The description

   a) Introduced

      In Acts 1:1, Luke wrote, "The former treatise have I made, O Theophilus, of all that Jesus began both to do and teach." He said that the book of Luke is about what Jesus began to do and that the book of Acts is about carrying on Jesus' work. Christ discipled the Twelve, and in the book of Acts we see them working with others. Two thousand years later, you and I are carrying on the work Jesus began. Jesus gave the baton to the apostles. They passed the baton on to others, and others have passed it on to us. We are to continue that succession: "The things that thou hast heard from me among many witnesses, the same commit thou to faithful men, who shall be able to teach others also" (2 Tim. 2:2). Every Christian is in a relay race. Each of us is to take the baton, then hand it on to others. None of us is in a solo effort. We're all in a flow of ministry. Somebody invested the gospel

118

in us, and we are to invest it in others—we are to be discipling others.

You may say, "I don't know much." Find someone that knows less than you do, and tell him what you know. Find someone that knows more than you do, and listen to him. Teach and be taught. I pour my heart into the people I disciple, and I learn from others. All of us have to be in that flow. We're not to be isolated; we're a chain all linked together.

b) Illustrated

In 1 Corinthians 4 are some verses that give us a wonderful, indirect insight into the discipling process. Paul was writing a letter of rebuke to the Corinthian church, which he himself brought into existence by the grace of God and the power of the Spirit. He was rebuking them because they had departed from the basics of the faith and were involved in sinful things. He wanted to correct them.

In verses 14-15, Paul writes, "I write not these things to shame you, but as my beloved sons I warn you. For though ye have ten thousand instructors [Gk., *paidagōgos,* 'moral guardians that give spiritual advice'] in Christ, yet have ye not many fathers; for in Christ Jesus I have begotten you through the gospel." He said that because the Corinthians were wondering what gave him the right to rebuke them. Paul explained why: He was their spiritual father. He had brought their church into existence. That brings us to the first element of discipleship:

(1) Evangelism

You can't have discipleship without having evangelism. If you don't evangelize, then you won't have anyone to disciple. The best way to begin discipling is to lead someone to Jesus Christ. When you do that, there will be a special link between you and the person you witnessed to. You may have strong links with other new believers, but there's something special about the link between a believer and the person that he brought to Christ. The new believer will have a sense of indebtedness, responsibility, and love toward you. It will be easier for you to say

sensitive things to someone you've led to Christ—things you would hestitate to say to others.
A new believer will have a special bond with you
if you were God's agent that brought him to
Christ. Now, each of us has probably discipled
someone that another person led to Christ. That
is wonderful, too. Discipleship begins with evangelism.

(2) Love

In 1 Corinthians 4:14, Paul calls the Corinthians
"my beloved sons." Discipleship is to be done
with an attitude of love. Now, love is not an
emotion; it's a commitment of self-sacrificing
humble service to a person with a need. Discipleship needs to take place in an environment of
love. You need to be able to say, "I'll give my life
and my time for you. I'll pray for you and give
you my insights." If you don't care about a
person and are not willing to make sacrifices for
him, then the discipling process will not reach its
richest potential.

(3) Admonishment

Paul told the Corinthians in verse 14, "I warn
you." The Greek word there is *noutheteō*, which
means "to admonish" or "to warn people to
change their behavior so that God won't chasten
them." Discipling is corrective. It starts with
bringing someone to Christ; it exists in an aura of
love, and it's marked by warning. It's just like
rearing a child. You have to warn your children
what to stay away from. You can't just give
children positive instruction; they need negative
instruction, too. Paul said to the Ephesian elders
at Miletus, "Therefore, watch, and remember,
that for the space of three years I ceased not to
warn everyone night and day with tears" (Acts
20:31). He knew the importance of admonishment. Someone asked me, "How important is a
ministry of warning?" I told him that it was
essential. When we're discipling someone, we
must be able to tell him what to do and what not
to do. That's a part of discipling.

(4) Guidance

This is the most important element in discipleship. Paul says in verse 16, "Wherefore, I beseech you, be ye followers of me." the person you are discipling is to follow your example. You say, "That's where I bail out! You mean I have to tell someone to be like me?" That's right. You have to be further along the path of spiritual development than the person you're discipling. You have to be able to provide leadership.

Our Lord isn't asking for perfection; it's direction He wants you to provide. He wants you to lead the person you are discipling in the right direction. Now I wouldn't be able to follow a perfect person; that would be too difficult. It's the imperfections of a person that help me understand the path that I'm supposed to walk. Discipling requires you to be an example. Paul said, "Be ye followers of me, even as I also am of Christ" (1 Cor. 11:1). Tell the person you are discipling, "I want you to follow me the way I'm following Christ." You don't say it proudly; you say it humbly, understanding your own weakness.

(5) Teaching

Paul mentions another element of discipleship in 1 Corinthians 4:17: "For this cause have I sent unto you Timothy, who is my beloved son and faithful in the Lord, who shall bring you into remembrance of my ways which are in Christ, as I teach everywhere in every church." Paul sent Timothy to teach the Corinthians. In discipleship, there has to be an imparting of divine truth. People function on truth. So, discipleship involves bringing a person to Christ, building a relationship of sacrificial love with him, admonishing him to change his behavior if it's going to bring God's chastening (or forfeiture of blessing), setting a model that he can follow, and filling him with the truth of God. That's why Paul talked to the Corinthians the way he did. In fact, he told them that if they didn't change their behavior, he would come to them with a rod (v. 21a). If they did change their behavior, then he would come to them in a spirit of love and meekness (v. 21*b*). Paul was rearing spiritual children. At Grace Church, we're committed to those principles of discipleship.

3. The dedication

Jesus said that when a man is fully discipled, he "shall be as his teacher" (Luke 6:40). We are to reproduce ourselves. One of the characteristics of life is reproduction. You're to pour yourself into other people, whether it be your spouse, your children, a friend, a person you led to Christ, or people in a class you teach. You're to invest your life in another person, and be accountable to him. If someone asks you, "Show me how I'm to live," then make sure your life is right so that you'll be the example you should be. Accountability is a good thing. First John 2:6 says, "He that saith he abideth in him ought himself also so to walk, even as he walked." Our model is Christ, and we're to nurture people in their walk with Christ.

Discipling is a function that everyone must be involved in. It isn't optional. We're all to bring people to the knowledge of the Savior and go through the process of developing them. We're all to disciple people that the Lord brings across our path. You will probably have different kinds of relationships with the people you disciple, but discipleship is nothing more than building a true friendship with a spiritual basis. It's not being friends with someone because you both like baseball, the same music, the same hobbies, or work at the same place. You're not friends because of a superficial thing; you're friends because at the core of your friendship is an openness about spiritual issues. That's what carries a discipling relationship along.

4. The destination

When you disciple someone, you're basically teaching him to live a godly life-style. You're teaching him biblical responses. A person is spiritually mature when his involuntary responses are godly. That's how to know if the Spirit of God has control in someone's life. In discipleship, you're to bring a person to the point where he doesn't have to figure out how to act right, but where he can react right spontaneously.

F. Shepherding

   1. The application of shepherding

Everybody in a church needs to care for one another. We must be involved in mutually caring for one another and meeting needs. Three times Jesus asked Peter, "Lovest thou me?" (John 21:15-17). Peter responded every time, "Yes, Lord; You know that I love You." Jesus said, "Then feed My sheep." He was saying, "You're a shepherd, Peter. Take care of My people."

Shepherding involves feeding and leading the flock. First Peter says, "Feed the flock of God which is among you, taking the oversight of it" (5:2a). Acts 20:28 says, "Take heed, therefore, unto yourselves, and to all the flock, over which the Holy Spirit hath made you overseers, to feed the church of God." We all are to care for one another. First John 3:17 says, "Whosoever hath this world's good, and seeth his brother have need, and shutteth up his compassions from him, how dwelleth the love of God in him?" How can you say you love God if you don't care about people? You have to be involved in the shepherding process. Each of you interacts with other people, and you've got to find out about other people's hurts and needs. If you have enough food on your plate to feed others and don't have any food, then share it. If you have insight that a wandering person needs, share it with him and lead him back. Everyone is to be in the shepherding process. First Peter 5:4 calls the Lord "the chief Shepherd." The implication is that we're His undershepherds. We're all involved in caring for the sheep.

   2. The availability in shepherding

Sometimes it's hard to shepherd people. Some people that have needs escape the notice of others or are overlooked. It always breaks my heart when someone tells me, "I was sick, and no one called me. No one cared." Sometimes I get letters from distraught people that say, "Such-and-such happened and you didn't call us. You didn't care. No one from the church helped us." My heart aches when I hear that. Sometimes people's expectations are too high; I can't be everywhere at one time. But most of the time people are overlooked because no one makes himself available when a need arises. For example, when someone has a death in his family, everybody immediately swarms around that person to comfort and support him. But after the funeral, when the real depression hits, that person is left alone. We lose our sensitive touch when it is most needed.

3. The activity of shepherding

We need to be the kind of shepherd that Jesus is. In John 10, He says, "I am the door of the sheep. . . . I am the good shepherd" (vv. 7*b*, 11*a*). Jesus was speaking of the way a shepherd cares for his sheep. When the sheep went into the fold at the end of a day, the shepherd would examine each one as it passed under the rod that he held across the entrance to the fold. If he found any bruises or scratches, he poured oil on them. Tht's what David was referring to in Psalm 23 when he said, "Thy rod and thy staff they comfort me. . . . Thou anointest my head with oil; my cup runneth over" (vv. 4*b*, 5*b*). The shepherd is to care for his sheep. That's his responsibility.

4. The accountability in shepherding

There are some wonderful people in our church that don't get shepherded because they're quiet about their needs. There are other people that are always living in sin, and they've got shepherds hovering about them all the time trying to help them. Sometimes we have committee meetings where eight elders will get together to figure out how to shepherd someone. For example, a man was unfaithful to his wife. We approached him several times about it, but he kept going back to his sin. We wondered, "What are we to do with him?" We prayerfully took the situation to God, because we didn't know what to do. We still shepherded him, even though he didn't want that. In the midst of that, there are quiet people in our congregation that have needs that aren't known about. That's why it's important for all of us to see ourselves as sheep and shepherds caring for one another. Church leaders can't be expected to handle all the shepherding needs themselves. We are accountable before God to care for one another. Grace Church is not my church; it's everyone's church. It's Christ's church. The Lord has made everyone at Grace Church the stewards of His church. Shepherding involves mutual caring, meeting needs, and making sure that we're all living right spiritually.

The first thing I did when I started pastoring at Grace Church was to develop a way that we could shepherd people. I knew we could feed them; I just wanted to make sure we could lead them, because a shepherd feeds the flock *and* leads it to Christlikeness.

G. Building Up Families

1. The persecution by Satan

I believe that God uses the family as a unit for passing on righteousness from one generation to the next. That is made clear in Deuteronomy 6:7, 20-25, where God ordains the family as the basic unit to preserve righteousness in the world and pass on His truths from generation to generation. However, Satan attacks whatever God has ordained to preserve righteousness.

Basically, Satan has attacked three things: the government, the church, and the family. Wherever God has ordained a government that punishes evildoers and does good to those that are right, Satan will assail it. Wherever there is a church that exalts Christ and proclaims the Word, the devil will attack. He doesn't want families to pass on righteousness; therefore, he tries to disintegrate them.

The three basic units of preservation in society are the government, the church, and the family. People say, "Do you think there is a conspiracy to ruin our government?" Yes, there is. Our society is going downward. Why? Because most of the people in our society are godless, and that makes them pawns that Satan can use to make our government system collapse. Some people say, "Do you think Satan is attacking the church?" Yes, he is. Some churches have become very liberal. The National Council of Churches has just published a "nonsexist" Bible. For example, they changed the phrase "the Son of God" to "the child of God." They have absolutely no concern about whether or not the Holy Spirit called Jesus "the Son of God." That attacks the church.

Satan is using the immoral, lust-filled society we live in to attack the family. He has made it hard for the family to survive. The church must preserve the family. We're committed to that as a function at Grace Church; we teach and disciple children and young people. I am thrilled when

I see men in our church discipling sixth-grade boys one on one. It's beautiful to see the adults of our church working with the younger people, because the younger people are responsible for preserving what they learn and giving it to the next generation. I want our young people to know God's standards for marriage and the family. I'm grateful that we have counselors, family ministries, a family center, and other things that work toward the preservation and edification of godly families in our church.

2. The preservation by the Spirit

Ephesians 5:18 says, "Be not drunk with wine, in which is excess, but be filled with the Spirit." Paul was talking about religious drunkenness: The cultists of his day thought that they could commune with their deities if they were intoxicated enough. They were like some peoples of the Orient and elsewhere who get high on drugs to commune with their gods. In their drunken stupor, they had lustful orgies with temple prostitutes and thought they were communing with the gods. But Paul said, "If you want to communicate with God, you can't do it through drunkenness. You have to be filled with the Spirit of God. That's how you commune with the living God."

When people are filled with the Spirit of God, they submit to one another. In a family situation, that means that wives will submit to their husbands, and husbands will submit to their wives by loving them with a nourishing, cherishing, and purifying love. Children will submit to their parents, and parents will submit to the needs of their children by not provoking them to wrath but by nurturing them and bringing them up in the ways of Christ. Submission flows from Spirit-filled lives. The church is to make sure that families are controlled by the Spirit of God so they can experience blessing from everyone's submissiveness. If everyone in a family is fighting for his own rights, then any possibility of meaningful relationships is destroyed.

The families of a church should uphold each other. They should help each other with their children; they should pray for each other's children. What is your reaction when you see unruly children? Do you pray for them? Do you help other parents by teaching their children proper behavior? A church must care for its families. That is one of its functions.

H. Training

The church is to equip people for ministry. Ephesians 4:11-12 says, "And he gave some, apostles; and some, prophets; and some, evangelists; and some, pastors and teachers; for the perfecting of the saints for the work of the ministry for the edifying of the body of Christ."

At Grace Church we're trying to train people for ministry. We don't only want to teach spiritual truths; we want to train people to use what they learn. For example, by taking a course in evangelism, people can take all the Bible verses they know and learn how to use them to present the gospel to unbelievers. That kind of course gives people new zeal, because then they know how to witness. If someone believes that God is calling him to become a missionary, we don't send him somewhere right away. We spend a few years training him so that when he does go out, he will be fully equipped. The church has to be constantly equipping people for ministry.

We have courses in our church for training people to eventually become deacons and elders. We have courses in evangelism, missions, and youth work. We have seminary courses on our campus and a Bible institute to train young people for ministry. We don't just want to give people general information; we want to prepare them for a specific ministry.

Children need to be trained so that they know how to be good parents and spouses. They need to know how to be good leaders. People need to be developed. They need to be trained so that they are useful. Training is essential; that's what equipping the saints is all about. Allow yourself to be trained for a ministry that is consistent with your giftedness.

I. Giving

1. The principle explained

How committed are you to giving? The Macedonians gave abundantly out of their deep poverty (2 Cor. 8:1-5). Giving has nothing to do with how much you have. People say, "If I had more, I would give more." That's not necessarily true, because giving is not a matter of how much you have; it's a matter of where your heart is. Paul says in 2 Corinthians 9:6, "He who soweth sparingly shall reap also sparingly; and he who soweth bountifully shall reap also bountifully." If you give a little, you will get back a little. If you give abundantly, you will receive back much. God returns to you interest on whatever you give. It's like investing with God. Jesus said, "Give, and it shall be given unto you; good measure, pressed down, and shaken together, and running over" (Luke 6:38a). God wants you to know that you can trust Him with your money. That's the reverse of what He's doing to you: He gives you money and asks you, "Can I trust you with this?" You must prove that He can trust you with the money He gives you by giving it back to Him.

How Well Do You Manage God's Possessions?

The best lesson you'll ever learn about stewardship is that you don't own anything. Everything you have belongs to God. The only reason you have anything is that you are to manage those possessions—you're to prove whether or not you are a worthy steward. If you can't manage what God has given you, then He won't give you "the true riches," according to Luke 16:11.

The things you have don't belong to you. When you trust them to God, you become free. Then all you have to do is manage those things. If you own something that someone else needs more than you do, then give it to him. That's the spirit of Acts 2:44-45: "And all that believed were together, and had all things common; and sold their possessions and goods, and parted them to all men, as every man had need."

2. The practice examined

   a) Giving meagerly

   Some people don't give at all. Other people give token amounts. I don't know why. The church doesn't really need their money. But the people that don't give miss the opportunity to be obedient and receive multiplied blessings.

   Some people give a little. They'll throw a couple of dollars in the offering plate each Sunday. Usually those that give minimally do so because they're spending their money on unnecessary earthly possessions. That's sad. I grieve for them. I want people to give generously so that they will be able to experience God's blessings. Don't throw God tokens. When King David wanted to buy a threshing floor so that he could build an altar on it to the Lord, the threshing floor was offered to David without charge. But in 2 Samuel 24:24 he says, "Nay, but I will surely buy it . . . at a price; neither will I offer burnt offerings to the Lord my God of that which doth cost me nothing."

b) Giving properly

How committed are we to giving? One man told me about a church that's one-half the size of Grace Church, yet it gets twice the money Grace Church does in its offerings. He asked me, "Why is that?" I said, "I don't know. If they're giving for the wrong motives or if they are giving legalistically, then they won't experience God's blessing. Their offerings are meaningless. But if they're giving abundantly from their hearts, then that's great!" 1 Corinthians 16:2 says, "Upon the first day of the week let every one of you lay by him in store, as God hath prospered him."

Giving is a function of the church. We are to give not just to support our own churches but to support God's work in the world. The ministry of a church should include a goal of advancing God's kingdom. Churches aren't supposed to try to amass a fortune. We are to be good stewards of the money God gives us for our own use and use the rest of it to train other people and reach others with the gospel. God gave, Christ gave. How can God's people in Christ's church not give?

J. Fellowshiping

Fellowship is essential. The word *fellowship* means "a common life together." In a way, it sums up the other functions we've talked about. Fellowshiping involves being together, loving each other, sharing life, and communing together. Fellowshiping includes listening to someone who has a burden, praying with someone who has a need, visiting someone in a hospital, sitting in a class or a Bible study, and even singing a hymn with someone you've never met. Fellowshiping also involves new Christians' sharing their joy and people' sharing prayer requests. It's having everything in common.

Do you fellowship? Do you open your life to others? Do you share your problems with others that have problems so that you can minister together? Be committed to fellowshiping!

The essential functions of the church are preaching, teaching, evangelism, missions, worshiping, praying, discipling, shepherding, building up families, training, giving, and fellowshiping. Are you involved in shepherding? Are you praying? Are you discipling someone? Are you helping build up the families in your church? Are you being trained for a ministry or training others? Are you giving? I ask myself those questions and say, "Lord, am I doing what You want me to do?" I want to be sensitive to the Spirit of God as He encourages me to be more faithful in everything. I want to use all my energy for God. Henry Martyn, a nineteenth-century missionary to India and Persia, said, "Let me burn out for God; I just want to go when I'm spent." I want to do my best in all that God wants me to do. Many Christians get involved in superficial things; they don't make any major investment in the functions of the church. Consequently, they have no sense of accomplishment. Eventually, God will hold them accountable for how they used their time.

IV. THE FLESH

It's not important what the flesh of a church is like. Using the body analogy, when a man looks at a church, he looks at what's on the outside; God looks at the heart (1 Sam. 16:7*b*). It's what's in the heart of a church that determines what the church is like. It's important that a church have a skeleton: it must be committed to a high view of God, the absolute priority of Scripture, doctrinal clarity, personal holiness, and spiritual authority. A church must have internal systems; certain spiritual attitudes must be present in it. A church must be committed to certain functions. But when a church has all those things, it doesn't really matter what it looks like on the outside or how its programs takes shape.

When God, by His wonderful grace, first brought me to Grace Church, I said, "God, I know that if we are what you want us to be, there will be no trouble ministering effectively." Sometimes after pastors visit Grace Church they try to implement the flesh of our church in their churches. But it won't work, because the flesh can't stand without a skeleton, and it can't live without the internal systems. Once a church has a skeleton, internal systems, and muscles, then the flesh will take form. The true beauty of a church comes from within. The flesh takes its form after all the things on the inside are right.

Life Centers on the Chruch

I believe that God has called Grace Church into existence and made it a unique place. Almost every Sunday at our reception for first-time visitors I meet people from other states. Recently

130

we had people from Michigan and Florida here. A typical conversation will go like this: The visitors will say, "We're from Michigan." I say, "How nice! Are you visiting here?" They'll say, "No, we moved here." I'll ask them why, and they'll say, "To come to this church." Then they'll say, "Do you know where we might be able to find a place to stay until we get a house and a job?" Why do they do that? One good response I've heard is, "We believe that life centers on the church, not the job." That gives me a lump in my throat and makes me realize the tremendous accountability we have before God to be the church He wants us to be. We want to be His church built His way for His glory.

Focusing on the Facts

1. Explain the three requirements of a servant detailed in 1 Corinthians 4:1-4 (see p. 115).
2. On what basis is God going to judge what kind of servant you were (1 Cor. 4:5; see p. 116)?
3. Define discipling (Matt. 28:19-20; see p. 118).
4. Explain what Paul was saying in 2 Timothy 2:2 (see pp. 118-19).
5. What are the five elements of the discipling process (see pp. 119-21)?
6. What is the best way to begin discipling someone (see p. 119)?
7. Describe the nature of the relationship between a new Christian and the person who led him to Christ. What is one advantage of that special relationship (see pp. 119-20)?
8. What attitude must you have when you are discipling someone? Define that attitude (see p. 120).
9. What does it mean to admonish someone (see p. 120)?
10. What do you need to be able to provide for the person you are discipling? Will your imperfections have a negative effect on your ability to do that? Explain (see p. 121).
11. What do you need to tell the person that you are discipling? How are you to communicate that (1 Cor. 11:1; see p. 121)?
12. In discipleship, there has to be an imparting of _____ _____ (see p. 121).
13. Discipleship is nothing more than building a true _____ with a _____ basis (see p. 122).
14. What are you basically doing when you disciple someone (see p. 122)?
15. What does shepherding involve? What does the fact that the Lord is called "the chief Shepherd" imply (1 Pet. 5:4; see p. 123)?
16. What is the most common reason that a person's need is overlooked (see p. 123)?

17. Who are responsible for shepherding the flock (see p. 124)?
18. What did God ordain the family to do, according to Deuteronomy 6:7, 20-25 (see p. 125)?
19. What is Satan using to attack the family? Who is to preserve the family (see p. 125)?
20. What kind of life does submission flow from? What does a family that practices submission experience? What is destroyed when there is no submission (see p. 126)?
21. For what must a church equip people? Why do people need to be developed (see p. 127)?
22. Explain what Paul is saying in 2 Corinthians 9:6. What must we prove to God? How (see pp. 127-28)?
23. What is the best lesson a person can learn about stewardship? Explain (see p. 128).
24. People who don't give miss out on what (see p. 128)?
25. What does 1 Corinthians 16:2 tell us about giving (see p. 129)?
26. What does *fellowship* mean? give some examples of fellowship (see p. 129).
27. Does it matter what form the flesh of a church takes? Explain (see p. 130).

Pondering the Principles

1. Look over the five elements of discipleship mentioned on pages 119-22. Take each element listed, and discuss what would happen to a discipling relationship if that element were missing. Seek to develop such a relationship, and be sure to utilize each element mentioned.

2. Are you involved in the shepherding process at your church? In the past month, how available have you been to the people in your Bible study or Sunday school group? Get the phone numbers and addresses of those in your Bible study or Sunday school group. Keep in contact with those people frequently enough so that if a need arises, you or others will be able to take care of it immediately.

3. Are you involved in preserving the families at your church? What can you do right now to minister to them? How can you help the children of your church to grow up to be godly men and women? What kind of example are you for them? Whenever you are with any of the children at your church, remember that you are responsible for helping them pass on righteousness to the following generation.

4. What is your attitude about giving? Why? Read 2 Corinthians 9:6-7. How should you give? What is your motive for giving? Ask God to help you give unselfishly with the desire to advance God's kingdom in the world.

8
The Anatomy of a Church— Part 8
(Christ: The Head of the Church)

Outline

Introduction

Review
I. The Skeleton
II. The Internal Systems
III. The Muscles
IV. The Flesh

Lesson
V. The Head
  A. The Savior of His Church
    1. The work of salvation expressed
      a) His name
      b) His blood
        (1) The ratifications of the Old Covenant
        (2) The requirement of both covenants
        (3) The ramifications of the New Covenant
      c) His resurrection
    2. The work of the Savior explained
      a) He loves His church
        (1) The precedence of His love
        (2) The permanence of His love
        (3) The preeminence of His love
      b) He builds His church
        (1) The originator of the church
        (2) The owner of the church
  B. The Shepherd of His Church
    1. He equips His church
      a) The process
      b) The power
      c) The passion

2. He intercedes for His church
   a) 1 John 2:1
   b) Hebrews 4:15
C. The Sovereign of His Church
   1. He rules His church
      a) Through the discipline of errant believers
      b) Through the discernment of elders
   2. He teaches His church
D. The Sanctifier of His Church
   1. The matter of purifying the church
   2. The methods of purifying the church

Conclusion

Introduction

This lesson concludes our study *The Anatomy of a Church*. We have now come to the most important part. We have already talked about the church as a body.

Review

I. THE SKELETON (see pp. 9-17)

II. THE INTERNAL SYSTEMS (see pp. 24-91)

III. THE MUSCLES (see pp. 96-130)

IV. THE FLESH (see p. 130)

No body would be complete without a head. In this lesson, I want us to learn from the Word of God about the Head of the body, who is the Lord Jesus Christ. We have already talked about what we should be doing in the church, and it wouldn't be right if we didn't talk about the Head of the church and what He is doing in His church. By the way, it is very comforting to know that in spite of all the mistakes we make and all the sins that beset us as we attempt to do the will of God, Christ is building His church.

Lesson

V. THE HEAD

In Ephesians 4, Paul said "We will in all things grow up into Him who is the Head, that is, Christ. From him the whole body, joined and held together by every supporting ligament, grows and builds itself up in love, as each part does its work" (vv. 15b-16, NIV*). In other words, we are to endeavor to do everything we can in the church, but it's the power of Christ that makes everything work. That is a divine paradox: We are to do everything with all our effort, yet it is God who accomplishes everything. It is a great comfort to know that when we fail, He succeeds. Christ is our Head; without Him we can do nothing (John 15:5b).

The passage I thought might be most helpful for us to examine is the majestic benediction that concludes the epistle to the Hebrews, that is, Hebrews 13:20-21. I want to use those verses as a base for our study of other New Testament passages that will enrich our understanding of the Lord's work for His church. Let's read them: "Now the God of peace, that brought again from the dead our Lord Jesus, that great Shepherd of the sheep, through the blood of the everlasting covenant, make you perfect in every good work to do his will, working in you that which is well-pleasing in his sight, through Jesus Christ, to whom be glory forever and ever. Amen."

That benediction summarizes the work of Christ. At the same time, it summarizes the message of the epistle to the Hebrews. The doxology is intended to praise the God of peace. The Lord is called *the God of peace* because He made peace with sinful men through the blood of Jesus Christ. For those of us who are saved, He was once the God of wrath and judgment, but now He is the God of peace.

Hebrews 13:20-21 delineates how He became the God of peace through the work of Jesus Christ. It starts with the affirmation that He is the God of peace and ends with the statement that He is to be glorified for ever and ever. God is glorified by the wonderful work of the Lord Jesus Christ.

What does Christ do for His church? First, He is:

A. The Savior of His Church

1. The work of salvation expressed

   Three things in this text point to the saving work of Christ in behalf of His church.

New International Version.

137

a) His name

Hebrews 13:20 mentions the Savior of the church: the "Lord Jesus." In Matthew 1:21 we read, "Thou shalt call his name *JESUS*, for he shall save his people from their sins." Jesus means "Jehovah saves." It is the Greek form of the Old Testament name *Joshua*. So, *Jesus* is the name of One who saves. Hebrews 2:9-10 says, "But we see Jesus, who was made a little lower than the angels for the suffering of death, crowned with glory and honor, that he, by the grace of God, should taste death for every man. For it became him, for whom are all things, and by whom are all things, in bringing many sons unto glory, to make the captain of their salvation perfect through sufferings." Jesus is the One who tasted death for every man. He became "the captain" [Gk., *archēgos*, "the pioneer" or "the beginner"] of salvation. He was made perfect in His own offering of Himself.

Acts 4:12 says, "There is no other name under heaven given among men, whereby we must be saved." Jesus' name speaks of His saving work.

b) His blood

(1) The ratifications of the Old Covenant

Our salvation was made possible by "the blood of the everlasting covenant" (v. 20). The Jewish people knew that sin had to be atoned for by blood. That's part of the message of the book of Hebrews. In Hebrews 9:18 we read, "Whereupon, neither the first testament was dedicated without blood." Every Jewish person knew that the ratification of the Old Covenant in Leviticus 17:11 was by blood. God required that there be bloodshed to deal with sin. Moses was God's agent to sprinkle the blood ratifying the Old Covenant: "For when Moses had spoken every precept to all the people according to the law, he took the blood of calves and of goats, with water, and scarlet wool, and hyssop, and sprinkled both the book, and all the people saying, This is the blood of the testament which God hath enjoined unto you. Moreover, he sprinkled with blood both the tabernacle and all the vessels of the ministry" (Heb. 9:19-21). There was blood everywhere: on the book of the law, on the people, on the Tabernacle, and on all the vessels in the Tabernacle.

(2) The requirement of both covenants

God was saying that there is no covenant made with Him without the shedding of blood. However, all of that bloodshed was only symbolic of the blood that would be shed by Christ to bring men peace with God. Hebrews 9:22 says, "Almost all things are by the law purged with blood, and without shedding of blood is no remission [forgiveness]." That's why Jesus had to shed His blood to ratify the New Covenant. He says in Matthew 26:28, "This is my blood of the new testament, which is shed for many for the remissions of sins." He was saying, in effect, "My blood will be the inaugurator of a new covenant."

Covenants were made in blood. If a man was to have peace with God, it had to be through the shedding of blood. Animal sacrifices couldn't bring that about; they were only a picture of the ultimate sacrifice of Christ, which brought true peace.

(3) The ramifications of the New Covenant

Notice that Hebrews 13:20 says, "The blood of the everlasting covenant." The Mosaic Covenant—the Old Covenant—was not everlasting. It was a temporary covenant; it was a shadow of things to come (Heb. 10:1). Jesus Christ made an everlasting covenant: "By one offering he hath perfected forever them that are sanctified" (Heb. 10:14). By one act of sacrifice, Christ brought an everlasting salvation. Hebrews 9:12 says, "Neither by the blood of goats and calves, but by his own blood he entered in once into the holy place, having obtained eternal redemption for us." Whereas the priests of Israel had to repeatedly make sacrifices in the holy place, Christ made one sacrifice and purchased eternal redemption for us (Heb. 10:11-12).

c) His resurrection

It is "the God of peace, that brought again from the dead our Lord Jesus. "When the Father raised Jesus from the dead, He was placing His stamp of approval on Jesus' finished work. We think of Christ's resurrection as a means to our own resurrection. That is true, but there's much more to it than that. We must look at the resurrection of Jesus Christ as the single greatest affirmation of the Father's approval of Jesus' saving work. When the Father raised Jesus from the dead, He was affirming that Jesus had accomplished what He had gone to the cross to do.

So, Hebrews 13:20 very clearly presents the saving work of Christ: Jesus, through His blood, brought us into an everlasting covenant. In response to the work that Jesus did, the God of peace raised Him from the dead. Paul says in Ephesians 2:14 that Christ is our peace. Colossians 1:20 says that Christ "made peace through the blood of his cross." That's why, according to Luke 10:6, a Christian is called "the son of peace."

Grace Church is not a human organization, nor is any church of Jesus Christ. You don't get into this church just by signing a card. You don't become a member simply because you like the people here, or think it might be good for business, or want to upgrade your life-style. You don't become a part of the church just because you like the music or the fun activities. You come into the church by virtue of the sacrificial death of the Lord Jesus Christ. Only those who are redeemed and washed with His precious blood belong to it. We're not building the church; He's building it. It's His church. He's the Savior of the church. And He brings people into it.

2. The works of the Savior explained

Christ does two things as the Savior of His church.

a) He loves His church

(1) The precedence of His love

Christ's saving work is built upon His saving love. We love Him because He first loved us (1 John 4:19). God predetermined a love relationship with us before we ever existed and loved us while we hated Him. Even when we were enemies, God, through His great love, reconciled us to Himself through the death of His Son. Christ loves us. His love redeemed us. It made Him give up His precious blood, which is more precious than any human commodity (1 Pet. 1:18-19).

Ephesians 5:2 says, "Walk in love, as Christ also hath loved us, and hath given himself for us an offering and a sacrifice to God for a sweet-smelling savor." Christ loved us so much that He gave Himself for us. It's wonderful to know you're loved. Those of us who are leaders in the church may be doing the best we can, yet people will still have unfulfilled needs and problems. We'll often say, "Lord, this is my life and passion; I care for this church! Things are not going the way they should!" However, our grief should be assuaged by the fact that Christ loves the church infinitely more than we do. My heart is comforted by the fact that even when I grieve over a person that is not living as he should, Christ is also grieved and still loves that person.

(2) The permanence of His love

Christ loves His church. John 13:1 says, "Having loved his own who were in the world, he loved them unto the end." He doesn't stop loving His people because they fail or fall. He doesn't stop loving His people when they are indifferent to Him or because they don't take advantage of their opportunities, resources, and privileges. The One who knows everything there is to know loves even the people He knows so well. We are comforted by the fact that He loves His church.

He determined to set His love upon us before the world began and will fulfill that until the world is reborn in the future. He who knew no sin loved us so much that He became sin for us, that we might be made the righteousness of God in Him (2 Cor. 5:21). Christ is at work in His church, loving people into it and loving them while they're in it. His love is rising as a fragrance to the nostrils of the Holy One (Eph. 5:2).

(3) The preeminence of His love

If Christ loves His church, then I need to love it, too. Because I know that He loves His church, I know that He is infinitely more concerned than I could be about what happens to it. If I think I have the right to be concerned about the church because I'm investing my life in it, how much more is Jesus concerned because He gave His life for it!

In Revelation 1:5-6 is a beautiful doxology: "Unto him that loveth us, and washed us from our sins in his own blood, and hath made us a kingdom of priests unto God." That's incomprehensible! The word *loveth* is in the present tense. Jesus loves His church. Paul said, "For I am persuaded that neither death, nor life, nor angels, nor principalities, nor powers, nor things present, nor things to come, nor height, nor depth, nor any other creation, shall be able to separate us from the love of God, which is in Christ Jesus, our Lord" (Rom. 8:38-39).

Christ loves His church. That's comforting to me. He loves the church far more than I do. That tells me that He will give His attention to the object of His love.

b) He builds His church

(1) The originator of the church

Since Christ is the One who saves people, He is the One who builds the church. He brought us into His church and adds others to it. He fitly frames the church together that it may grow as a holy temple to Himself (Eph. 2:21). I love what He says in Matthew 16:18: "I will build my church." What a great thought! We aren't in the church-building business; He is. It's not my job to build the church, and it's not your job, either. We are not to use human wisdom or methods to build the church. Christ will build the church, "and the gates of hades shall not prevail against it" (Matt. 16:18*b*). The phrase *gates of hades* is a Hebrew euphemism for death (see Rev. 1:18). Death is the ultimate weapon that's in the hand of the adversary (Heb. 2:14). Who has the power of death? Satan. In Matthew 16:18, Jesus is saying, "I will build My church, and even killing the saints won't prevail against it." If Satan kills those in the church, then he is just populating glory!

I want to be a part of the church that Christ is building. That's why I'm committed to the fact that we must go by the Bible. We don't want to be using human devices to build the church, because then we won't know whether we did it or He did it. I just want to be a part of what He's doing.

(2) The owner of the church

I love what He says in Matthew 16:18: He doesn't say, "I will build *the* church"; He says, "I will build *my* church." What a great truth! He is the possessor of the church. People often ask me, "Who owns your church?" The Lord Jesus Christ does! He purchased it with His own precious blood. He owns it, and He builds it. In fact, He adds to the church daily those who are to be saved (Acts 2:47*b*). He's in the church-building business.

In John 10:27, Jesus says, "My sheep hear my voice, and I know them, and they follow me." We belong to Him. He's the builder, owner, purchaser, chief cornerstone, and foundation of the church. The church is His. It's being built and He has promised that it cannot fail. Opposition, threats, carnality, human ineptitude, indifference, apostasy, liberalism, and denominationalism will not prevail against the church. Christ is building His church.

First Corinthians 3:9 says, "Ye are God's building." Ephesians 2:21-22 says that you've been built into a holy temple in the Lord, "in whom ye also are built together for an habitation of God through the Spirit." Paul told Timothy, "These things write I unto thee . . . that thou mayest know how thou oughtest to behave thyself in the house of God, which is the church" (1 Tim. 3:14*a*, 15). The church belongs to the Lord.

Christ is the Savior of His church. He loves it and builds it.

B. The Shepherd of His Church

Hebrews 13:20 calls the Lord the "great Shepherd of the sheep." That's a lovely thought. As the Shepherd, He has some unique functions.

First, I want you to note that He's the Great Shepherd, in contrast to all other shepherds. Psalm 77:20 says, "Thou didst lead thy people like a flock by the hand of Moses and Aaron." Moses and Aaron were shepherds but not Great Shepherds. Jesus is called *shepherd* three times in the New Testament: In John 10:11, He's the "good shepherd"; in 1 Peter 5:4, He's the "chief Shepherd"; and in Hebrews 13:20, He's the "great Shepherd." In several places the Bible refers to ungodly people as sheep without a shepherd (Num. 27:17; 1 Kings 22:17; 2 Chron. 18:16; Ezek. 34:5, 8; Zech. 10:2; Matt. 9:36; Mark 6:34). Believers are sheep with a shepherd.

Relying on the Great Shepherd

At a recent meeting of the leaders at Grace Church, we were discussing how we can develop a better way to shepherd the people in our church. Some were saying, "Certain people are not getting involved, and others are not following through on their responsibilities. We've lost contact with some people, and there are others who have been gone for a long time that we're trying to track down." When I leave a meeting like that, I think, "Lord, how are we going to keep track of the people we have? How can we better shepherd them?" Sometimes people become ill, and we don't know about it, or a tragedy happens. There are people that we haven't been able to talk with to assess their relationship with the Lord. I find myself frequently wondering how we can shepherd the sheep. But all of us can take comfort in this: The Great Shepherd is shepherding His sheep. Sometimes when a saved person doesn't get into a follow-up program, we act as though he will lose his salvation. We say, "We have to help the Holy Spirit along. We can't just leave people up to the Lord. We've got to get them into a program." It's good to watch over and help God's people, but we must remember that the Lord is the Shepherd. I'm not going to worry about His sheep. I want to be faithful to the sheep He has entrusted to my care, and I'll do all that I can to help them, but they're His sheep.

I wouldn't be able to maintain my sanity if I felt I were ultimately responsible for Christ's sheep. My whole heart is into what I'm doing for His sheep, but that's not because I think it all depends on me. Christ will build his church with or without us. If the gates of hell can't prevail against it, then we certainly can't. Our service to Christ is not to do what He can't do; it's to be a part of what He is doing. At Grace Church we serve the Lord with our whole heart, but when we run out of resources and don't know what to do to meet people's needs, we can lean back and say, "The Lord is the Great Shepherd."

Recently, a woman in our church died when she gave birth to a child. The baby was premature and had to be put on life support systems. It had also been without oxygen to the brain for a short period of time. Imagine the situation the father was in. We thought, *What can we say?* But we can fall back on the fact that the Great Shepherd takes care of His sheep. That's where human resources come to an end. The Lord is the Great Shepherd, the chief Shepherd, and the good Shepherd.

As the great Shepherd, the Lord does two things.

1. He equips His church

    a) The process

In Hebrews 13:21, we read that the Great Shepherd, through the blood of the everlasting covenant, "[makes] you perfect in every good work to do his will." The reason He perfected us in salvation was to cause us to do His will. He's perfecting and equipping us to do His will. He uses His Word to shape us. All Scripture was given by God so "that the man of God may be perfect, thoroughly furnished unto all good works" (2 Tim. 3:17). He's given us His Word, and He's given us gifted men to help equip us: "He gave some, apostles; and some, prophets; and some, evangelists; and some, pastors and teachers; for the perfecting of the saints" (Eph. 4:11-12*a*).

There is another way that we are perfected: 1 Peter 5:10 says that after we have suffered a while, the Lord will make us perfect. He gives us trials so that the Word can work in our lives. John 15:2-3 says that the Word prunes us.

God gave us the Scriptures and brought us gifted men to equip us. He also gives us trials and suffering. Why? Because that's what forces us to apply the Word. That's the refining process. When you struggle with sin and suffering, you see boiling up within you the ugliness of your own sin. As a result, you learn to hate sin more. Those are the times you may question God and have doubts. Through those times, you'll learn to hate your own sinfulness and doubts.

145

Those are the times when you will long for heaven and deliverance from this world. Suffering does good things for you. The Lord brings suffering into people's lives.

b) The power

The Lord equips, builds up, and strengthens us. He gives us the power of the Holy Spirit. He said, "Ye shall receive power, after the Holy Spirit is come upon you; and ye shall be witnesses unto me both in Jerusalem, and in all Judea, and in Samaria, and unto the uttermost part of the earth" (Acts 1:8). In John 15:16 He says that we would go forth and bear much fruit, and in John 7:38 He says, "Out of [your] heart shall flow rivers of living water." Christ is equipping His church.

The Privilege of Participating in Christ's Work

At Grace Church, we're involved in training people. We disciple and evangelize others. We're working as hard as we can, continually remembering that the Lord is equipping His church. He's doing that through the Word, through trials, and through the power of the Spirit of God. We're not doing those things because the church depends on us; we're doing them because we want to be a part of what He's doing. I can't think of a greater privilege.

c) The passion

Ephesians 5:29 is a verse that is normally used to speak of marriage, but beyond that it speaks of the church: "No man ever yet hated his own flesh, but nourisheth and cherisheth it, even as the Lord the church." The Lord nourishes and cherishes the church. *Nourish* means "to feed." *Cherish* means "to warm with body heat." The term *cherish* is used to speak of a nursing mother in 1 Thessalonians 2:7. In a sense, then, Ephesians 5:29 is saying that the Lord nurtures His beloved church. That speaks of intimacy. The Lord cherishes us—He warms us with His body heat to melt or soften us. The Lord shepherds, feeds, and warms us; He melts us down to reshape us.

Christ is at work in His church. Sometimes I get frustrated and say, "Lord, how can we get people more committed? How can we make them more equipped and get them growing?" But I'm comforted by the fact that He is taking care of that. He's equipping, nourishing, and cherishing His church.

2.   He intercedes for His church

Like a shepherd would protect his sheep by fighting off a wolf, the Lord Jesus Christ fights off the adversary who constantly comes before the throne of God to accuse Christians. Satan accuses us as he accused Job (Job 1:7-12; 2:1-5). However, Jesus comes to our rescue. He is our defender, intercessor, advocate, and sympathizer. He is our High Priest. In John 17:9, 11, He says, "I pray not for the world, but for them whom thou hast given me; for they are thine. . . . Holy Father, keep through thine own name those whom thou hast given me, that they may be one, as we are." Jesus prays for those who belong to Him in that marvelous passage. His high-priestly work can be seen elsewhere in the New Testament:

a)   1 John 2:1

John said, "If any man sin, we have an advocate with the Father, Jesus Christ the righteous." In other words, when you sin and accusation is brought before the throne of God, Jesus stands as your advocate and says, "Father, My blood paid for that sin." That's why no sin can be charged against God's elect (Rom. 8:33-34). Is God going to charge your sin against you when he has already justified you? Is there some information that He didn't have previously that will go against you? Is there a higher court than God? Will Christ condemn you when He already bore your sin in His own body on the cross? Will He who perfectly expiated all your sin hold any sin against you? Never! Christ always intercedes for those that are in His church. He talks to the Father about our needs, too, because we have many needs.

b)   Hebrews 4:15

The writer of Hebrews said, "For we have not an high priest who cannot be touched with the feeling of our infirmities, but was in all points tempted like as we are, yet without sin." Christ knows exactly what we go through, so He's able to help us (Heb. 2:18). He is a perfect High Priest: "He ever liveth to make intercession for [us]" (Heb. 7:25*b*). He experienced hunger, thirst, and fatigue. Christ was loved and hated. He was raised in a family. He was taught. He loved, hated, and marveled. Our Lord was glad, sad, angry, sarcastic, and grieved. He was overcome by future events (such as His crucifixion). Christ exercised faith, read Scripture, and prayed all night. He poured out His heart over the pain of man and wept when His own heart ached. The Lord has been through what we've been through. He's sympathetic, and He defends us. Christ is our faithful High Priest, always interceding for us.

As our Shepherd, He nurtures, cherishes, and equips us to do His will. He also intercedes as High Priest on our behalf, making sure that no sin is charged against us. His blood keeps on cleansing us from all sin (1 John 1:9).

C. The Sovereign of His Church

Looking again at our text, Hebrews 13:20-21, notice the word *Lord* in verse 20. The Greek word *kurios* is used ninety-two times in the New Testament. There are various meanings of the word, but when it is used in the New Testament in reference to the Son of God, it means "sovereign One," or "One who is in complete authority." He is the Lord—the Sovereign—of His church. Ephesians 1:22-23 says that God "hath put all things under his feet, and gave him to be the head over all things to the church, which is his body, the fullness of him that filleth all in all." Christ is in charge.

Colossians 1:18-19 says the same thing: "He is the head of the body, the church; who is the beginning, the first-born [Gk., *prōtotokos* 'the preeminent One'] . . . that in all things he might have the pre-eminence. For it pleased the Father that in him should all fullness dwell."

The concept of Lord has to do with the fact that Jesus Christ is sovereign. The Lord manifests His sovereignty in the church in two ways.

1. He rules His church

As Lord of His church, He is its ruler. If anyone asks us who is in charge of Grace Church, we tell him, "Jesus Christ." Ephesians 5:23 says, "Christ is the head of the church." The word *head* is the Greek word *kephalē*, which speaks of being first, prominent, or supreme. As the Head, He has all the authority in His church.

a) Through the discipline of errant believers

In Revelation 1:12-15, we see Christ moving among candlesticks, which represent His church. He has feet like fine bronze and burning, penetrating eyes that search out, the sin that needs to be removed from His church. That's why Jesus says in Matthew 18:20, "For where two or three are gathered together in my name, there am I in the midst of them." Jesus wasn't talking about His presence at a prayer meeting; He was talking about being with two or three witnesses that confirm the sin of someone in the discipline process. The whole passage is about discipline. Jesus said, "Don't hesitate to discipline people. When you've called together the right witnesses and affirmed the sin, I'm there in your midst disciplining with you." You are only binding on earth what has been bound in heaven and loosing on earth whatever has already been loosed in heaven (Matt. 18:18). You act in behalf of Christ.

b) Through the discernment of elders

Christ rules His church. He rules through a plurality of godly men, or elders. At Grace Church, we have nearly fifty elders, and our one goal is to do what Christ wants us to do. We know most of what He wants to do because it's written in the Bible. When the Scripture is silent about a certain issue, then it's up to us to discern the mind of God prayerfully, thoughtfully, and patiently. We wait until God shows us what He wants us to do. That's why we've always been committed to unanimous agreement on a matter. God only has one will, so we know we have to be unanimous. It's up to all of us who are undershepherds to know what His will is. We seek His mind until we come to an understanding of His will.

I don't want that responsibility, nor would any individual in his right mind. It's hard enough to answer for your own life without having to answer for a host of others. So, as a group, we seek the mind of God through prayer until the Spirit of God reveals His will. He is the ruler of the church, and all we want to do is discern His will. That's why we follow the Bible so closely— it guides us.

2. He teaches His church

   Christ teaches His church; that's part of His ruling. He exercises authority in all matters and has authority to teach all truth. He's our Teacher. His will is revealed through His Word and through human instruments, but He is the Teacher. In fact, He told the disciples that several times in the gospel of John (14:20, 26; 15:26; 16:7, 12-14). In John 14:20, Jesus says, "Ye shall know that I am in my Father, and ye in me, and I in you." How are you going to know that? Verse 26 says, "The Comforter, who is the Holy Spirit, whom the Father will send in my name, he shall teach you all things, and bring all things to your remembrance, whatever I have said unto you."

   In John 15:26, Jesus says, "When the Comforter is come, whom I will send unto you from the Father, even the Spirit of truth, who proceedeth from the Father, he shall testify of me." In other words, "The Spirit will tell you what you need to know about Me." In addition, Jesus said, "I have yet many things to say unto you, but ye cannot bear them now. Nevertheless, when he, the Spirit of truth, is come, he will guide you into all truth; for he shall not speak of himself, but whatever he shall hear, that shall he speak; and he will show you things to come. He shall glorify me; for he shall receive of mine, and shall show it unto you" (John 16:12-14).

The Lord rules and teaches His church through the Word, the Spirit, and gifted men of God. We have the Word of God and the Spirit to help us. First John 2:20 says that we can draw on the Spirit for knowledge. Verse 27 says that we have an anointing from God; we don't need worldly, human teachers who don't know the Scriptures. As a pastor, I'm not to give you my own opinion. I'm not to talk about social issues that aren't related to the Word of God. I'm to open to you the Word of God so that you may know the mind of God and the heart of the Savior. Christ is the Teacher. I'm only a waiter. I didn't cook the meal; I'm only supposed to deliver it to you hot and without spoiling it.

Christ is not only the Savior who loves and builds His church, the Shepherd who equips and intercedes for His church, and the Sovereign who rules and teaches His church; He is also:

D. The Sanctifier of His Church

   Christ is the sanctifier who purifies and glorifies His church. According to Hebrews 13:21, Christ is "working in you." It's good to know that He is working in us. He's the sanctifier. Christ is the One who sets us apart from sin. He's the One who purifies us and leads us to give Him glory forever.

1. The matter of purifying the church

    When you see a Christian who has sin in his life, I'm sure that you feel concern for him. You want to see him free of it. Sometimes when you confront such a person, the discipline process goes on and on. When you have a situation like that, the only comfort you have is knowing that Christ is the purifier of His church.

2. The methods of purifying the church

    If the person you are disciplining is a Christian, then Christ may purify His church by removing him. He may cause the death of a believer who is unfaithful (1 Cor. 11:27-30; see also 1 John 5:16).

    Christ may also purify His church by strengthening a sinning Christian and bringing him into holiness. Ephesians 5:25-26 says, "Christ . . . loved the church, and gave himself for it, that he might sanctify and cleanse it with the washing of water by the word." Christ wants His church pure, so that ultimately "he might present it to himself a glorious church, not having spot, or wrinkle, or any such thing; but that it should be holy and without blemish" (v. 27).

Christ is the purifier and glorifier of His church. Glorification is simply ultimate purification. Someday, we will be to the praise of the glory of God. Through Jesus Christ, the God of peace will receive glory forever and ever from us (Jude 25). Christ is at work purging us. It's so comforting to know that. He's also bringing us to glory. When we get to heaven, we'll be without blemish.

Conclusion

I hope it's as helpful for you to hear these things as it is to me. It's comforting to know that Christ hasn't left us with the responsibility of building His church. Let me repeat a key thought I mentioned earlier: We're not doing what Christ can't do. We're not building the church because He needs us to build it. If Grace Church blew up today, the church of Jesus Christ would move ahead. If all the leaders of Grace Church dropped dead, the church would still grow. Christ does not need us to build His church.

You say, "Then why are we to work so hard?" Because there's nothing more marvelous, thrilling, glorious, joy-producing, and soul-satisfying than to be a part of what Jesus Christ is building for His eternal glory!

Focusing on the Facts

1. What three things in Hebrews 13:20 point to the saving work of Christ in behalf of His church (see pp. 135-38)?
2. What does the name *Jesus* mean? What does Acts 4:12 say about the name of Jesus (see p. 136)?
3. How must sin be atoned for (see p. 136)?
4. The bloodshed in the Old Testament symbolized what (see p. 137)?
5. Was the Old Covenant permanent? Support your answer with Scripture. What did Christ obtain for us after He entered once into the Holy Place (Heb. 9:12; see p. 137)?
6. What was the single greatest affirmation of the Father's approval of Jesus' saving work (see p. 138)?
7. What is Christ's saving work built upon? What was Christ willing to do for us (1 Pet. 1:18-19; see pp. 138-39)?
8. Does Christ ever stop loving His people? Support your answer with Scripture (see p. 139).
9. What did Paul say could not separate us from the love of Christ (Rom. 8:38-39; see p. 140)?
10. Who is building the church? Explain the significance of the phrase "the gates of hades shall not prevail against [the church]" (Matt. 16:18*b*; see pp. 140-41).
11. How do we know who owns the church? Support your answer with different verses (see p. 141).
12. Jesus is called the _____ Shepherd (John 10:11), the _____ Shepherd (1 Pet. 5:4), and the _____ Shepherd (Heb. 13:20; see p. 142).
13. Explain the different ways Christ equips us to do His will (see p. 143).
14. What are trials and suffering good for? Why (see pp. 143-44)?
15. What is the source of our power to do God's will (see p. 144)?
16. What do the words *nourish* and *cherish* tell us about the nature of the relationship between Christ and His sheep (Eph. 5:29; see p. 144)?
17. As our intercessor, what does Jesus defend us from (see p. 145)?
18. Why can't a sin be charged against God's elect (see p. 145)?
19. What did the writer of Hebrews mean when he said, "For we have not an high priest who cannot be touched with the feeling

of our infirmities, but was in all points tempted like as we are, yet without sin (Heb. 4:15; see pp. 145-46)?

20. What does the word *Lord* mean in Hebrews 13:20? Using Scripture, support the fact that Christ is sovereign over the church (see p. 146).

21. Explain the two ways that Christ rules His church (see pp. 147-48).

22. What agent is Christ using to teach His church (John 14:26)? What did Christ say that agent would do (John 16:13-14; see p. 148)?

23. In what two ways does Christ purify His church? Why does Christ want His church pure (Eph. 5:27; see p. 149)?

24. If Christ does not need us to build His church, then why should we work so hard for it (see p. 150)?

Pondering the Principles

1. A human body is dependent upon its head for survival. Without the head, muscles would not coordinate, nerves would not be able to process their information, and glands would not secrete properly. Without the brain, the body would have no guidance. Describe in your own words what the church would be like without guidance from Christ. Include some thoughts on how preaching, teaching, discipling, caring for others' needs, and submission to spiritual authorities would be affected.

2. Imagine all the signals that are relayed through the nervous system from the various muscles of the body to the brain and back again when a baseball player swings his bat. While he is swinging, his eyes follow the ball, picking up information for the brain, which continually tells the muscles of the arms, hands, shoulders, and torso what to do. If the ballplayer were to develop a disease that destroyed his nervous system or muscles, then his body would no longer be able to cooperate with the commands of the brain. Using that picture, explain why it is important that *every* person (including you) in the Body of Christ purge himself from sin and "be a vessel unto honor, sanctified, and fit for the master's use, and prepared unto every good work" (2 Tim. 2:21).

3. Hebrews 13:20 calls the Lord the "great Shepherd of the sheep." Ephesians 5:29 speaks of the fact that Christ nourishes and cherishes those that are in His church. Read John 10:2-4, 9, 11, 14, and 28. According to those verses, what does Christ do for His sheep? Make a list of specific things the Great Shepherd has done for you, and thank Him for those things.

4. Do you submit to the authority of the government? Why does the government need to make laws for society? Describe the consequences you would suffer for breaking the law in each of the following ways: speeding, stealing, lying in court, counterfeiting money, and murdering. As a Christian, do you submit to the authority of Christ in the church? Are there things you are doing now that violate how Jesus commanded for you to live? Mention several different possible spiritual or physical consequences you would suffer if you didn't submit completely to Christ's rule. Make sure that you, as a part of the body of Christ, have made Christ sovereign in every area of your life.

Scripture Index